SO-BII-221

PROCESSING NEW INFORMATION

CLASSROOM TECHNIQUES TO HELP STUDENTS ENGAGE WITH CONTENT

PROCESSING NEW INFORMATION

CLASSROOM TECHNIQUES TO HELP STUDENTS ENGAGE WITH CONTENT

Tzeporaw Sahadeo-Turner
Robert J. Marzano

With Gwendolyn L. Bryant and Kelly Harmon

Learning Sciences
MARZANO
C E N T E R

Copyright © 2015 by Learning Sciences International

All rights reserved. Tables, forms, and sample documents may be reproduced or displayed only by educators, local school sites, or nonprofit entities who have purchased the book. Except for that usage, no part of this book may be reproduced, transmitted, or displayed in any form or by any means (photo-copying, digital or electronic transmittal, electronic or mechanical display, or other means) without the prior written permission of the publisher.

1400 Centrepark Blvd, Suite 1000
West Palm Beach, FL 33401
717-845-6300

email: pub@learningsciences.com
learningsciences.com

Printed in the United States of America

20 19 18 17 16 15   2 3 4

FSC
www.fsc.org
MIX
Paper from
responsible sources
FSC® C005010

Publisher's Cataloging-in-Publication Data

Sahadeo-Turner, Tzeporaw.
  Processing new information : classroom techniques to help students engage with content / Tzeporaw Sahadeo-Turner [and] Robert J. Marzano.
     pages cm. – (Essentials for achieving rigor series)
  ISBN: 978-1-941112-03-8 (pbk.)
1. Learning, Psychology of. 2. Learning strategies. 3. Critical pedagogy. 4. Effective teaching—United States. 5. Classroom management. I. Marzano, Robert J. II. Title.
  LB1060 .S23 2015
  370.15`23—dc23
                          [2014939269]

MARZANO CENTER

Essentials for Achieving Rigor SERIES

The *Essentials for Achieving Rigor* series of instructional guides helps educators become highly skilled at implementing, monitoring, and adapting instruction. Put it to practical use immediately, adopting day-to-day examples as models for application in your own classroom.

Books in the series:

Identifying Critical Content: Classroom Techniques to Help Students Know What is Important

Examining Reasoning: Classroom Techniques to Help Students Produce and Defend Claims

Recording & Representing Knowledge: Classroom Techniques to Help Students Accurately Organize and Summarize Content

Examining Similarities & Differences: Classroom Techniques to Help Students Deepen Their Understanding

Processing New Information: Classroom Techniques to Help Students Engage With Content

Revising Knowledge: Classroom Techniques to Help Students Examine Their Deeper Understanding

Practicing Skills, Strategies & Processes: Classroom Techniques to Help Students Develop Proficiency

Engaging in Cognitively Complex Tasks: Classroom Techniques to Help Students Generate & Test Hypotheses Across Disciplines

Creating & Using Learning Targets & Performance Scales: How Teachers Make Better Instructional Decisions

Organizing for Learning: Classroom Techniques to Help Students Interact Within Small Groups

"Live as if you were to die tomorrow. Learn as if you were to live forever."

—Mahatma Gandhi

Table of Contents

Acknowledgments

We always have more to learn, and we always have more reasons to learn. I want to thank my Gentle Giant, my husband, Cooper Jerome Turner III; my beautiful children Cierra, Caleb, and Cooper; and my family for allowing me to learn more so I can help other children in their endeavors to learn.

Writing a book is a legacy. It lives forever.

—Tzeporaw

Learning Sciences International would like to thank the following reviewers:

Amy Abrams
2014 Puget Sound Regional Teacher
 of the Year
Northwood Middle School
Renton, Washington

Julie Lima Boyle
2012 Rhode Island Teacher
 of the Year
Coventry High School
Coventry, Rhode Island

Michael Funkhouser
2013 West Virginia Teacher
 of the Year
East Hardy High School
Baker, West Virginia

Anne E. Hasse
2014 Wisconsin Elementary Teacher
 of the Year
Wakanda Elementary School
Menomonie, Wisconsin

Daniele Massey
2013 Teacher of the Year
Department of Defense Education
 Activity

Katie Perez
2014 Kansas Regional Teacher
 of the Year
Morgan Elementary
Hutchinson, Kansas

Stephanie Seay
2006 South Carolina State Teacher
 of the Year
Cannons Elementary
Spartanburg, South Carolina

Kathleen M. Turner
2013 Massachusetts Teacher
 of the Year
Sharon High School
Sharon, Massachusetts

About the Authors

TZEPORAW SAHADEO-TURNER, MSEd, MS, has made effective pedagogy and student achievement the primary focuses of her career. Her history as a high school science teacher, an eighth-grade comprehensive science teacher, and an administrator with both Florida's Hillsborough County and the Florida Virtual School has allowed her to experience and evaluate effective curricula and pedagogy from nearly every angle. She earned both of her master's degrees from the University of South Florida.

ROBERT J. MARZANO, PhD, is CEO of Marzano Research Laboratory and Executive Director of the Learning Sciences Marzano Center for Teacher and Leader Evaluation. A leading researcher in education, he is a speaker, trainer, and author of more than 150 articles on topics such as instruction, assessment, writing and implementing standards, cognition, effective leadership, and school intervention. He has authored over 30 books, including *The Art and Science of Teaching* (ASCD, 2007) and *Teacher Evaluation That Makes a Difference* (ASCD, 2013).

GWENDOLYN L. BRYANT, MSEd, has taught learning disability, preschool, elementary, middle school, and college levels. Before becoming a staff developer with Learning Sciences International, Gwendolyn designed content and served as a district-level lead teacher and middle school improvement and literacy coach.

KELLY HARMON, MAEd, is a national presenter who has more than 20 years of experience working with at-risk students. She presents on a wide range of topics including response to intervention (RTI), technology, reading, writing, and strategies for highly effective teachers.

Introduction

This guide, *Processing New Information: Classroom Techniques to Help Students Engage with Content*, is intended as a resource for improving a specific element of instructional practice: processing new information. Active processing results in students' abilities to summarize, make predictions, ask clarifying questions, and discuss chunks of critical content. Processing new information is vital to engaging students in more rigorous learning.

Your motivation to incorporate this strategy into your instructional toolbox may have come from a personal desire to improve your instructional practice through the implementation of a research-based set of strategies (such as those found in the Marzano instructional framework) or a desire to increase the rigor of the instructional strategies you implement in your classroom so that students meet the expectations of demanding standards such as the Common Core State Standards, Next Generation Science Standards, C3 Framework for Social Studies State Standards, or state standards based on or influenced by College and Career Readiness Anchor Standards.

This guide will help teachers of all grade levels and subjects improve their performance of a specific instructional strategy: processing new information. Narrowing your focus on a specific skill, such as processing new information, allows you to concentrate on the nuances of this instructional strategy to deliberately improve it. This allows you to intentionally plan, implement, monitor, adapt, and reflect on this single element of your instructional practice. A person seeking to become an expert displays distinctive behaviors, as explained by Marzano and Toth (2013):

- breaks down the specific skills required to be an expert

- focuses on improving those particular critical skill chunks (as opposed to easy tasks) during practice or day-to-day activities

- receives immediate, specific, and actionable feedback, particularly from a more experienced coach

- continually practices each critical skill at more challenging levels with the intention of mastering it, giving far less time to skills already mastered

This series of guides will support each of the previously listed behaviors, with a focus on breaking down the specific skills required to be an expert and giving day-to-day practical suggestions to enhance these skills.

Building on the Marzano Instructional Model

This series is based on the Marzano instructional framework, which is grounded in research and provides educators with the tools they need to connect instructional practice to student achievement. The series uses key terms that are specific to the Marzano model of instruction. See Table 1, Glossary of Key Terms.

Table 1: Glossary of Key Terms

Term	Definition
CCSS	Common Core State Standards is the official name of the standards documents developed by the Common Core State Standards Initiative (CCSSI), the goal of which is to prepare students in the United States for college and career.
CCR	College and Career Readiness Anchor Standards are broad statements that incorporate individual standards for various grade levels and specific areas.
Desired result	The intended result for the student(s) due to the implementation of a specific strategy.
Monitoring	The act of checking for evidence of the desired result of a specific strategy while the strategy is being implemented.
Instructional strategy	A category of techniques used for classroom instruction that has been proven to have a high probability of enhancing student achievement.
Instructional technique	The method used to teach and deepen understanding of knowledge and skills.
Content	The knowledge and skills necessary for students to demonstrate standards.
Scaffolding	A purposeful progression of support that targets cognitive complexity and student autonomy to reach rigor.
Extending	Activities that move students who have already demonstrated the desired result to a higher level of understanding.

The educational pendulum swings widely from decade to decade. Educators move back and forth between prescriptive checklists and step-by-step lesson plans to approaches that encourage instructional autonomy with minimal regard for the science of teaching and need for accountability. Two practices are often missing in both of these approaches to defining effective instruction: 1) specific statements of desired results, and 2) solid research-based connections. The Marzano instructional framework provides a comprehensive system that details what is required from teachers to develop their craft using research-based instructional strategies. Launching from this solid instructional foundation, teachers will then be prepared to merge that science with their own unique, yet effective, instructional style, which is the art of teaching.

Processing New Information: Classroom Techniques to Help Students Engage with Content will help you grow into an innovative and highly skilled teacher who is able to implement, scaffold, and extend instruction to meet a range of student needs.

Essentials for Achieving Rigor

This series of guides details essential classroom strategies to support the complex shifts in teaching that are necessary for an environment where academic rigor is a requirement for all students. The instructional strategies presented in this series are essential to effectively teach the CCSS, the Next Generation Science Standards, or standards designated by your school district or state. They require a deeper understanding, more effective use of strategies, and greater frequency of implementation for your students to demonstrate the knowledge and skills required by rigorous standards. This series includes instructional techniques appropriate for all grade levels and content areas. The examples contained within are grade-level specific and should serve as models and launching points for application in your own classroom.

Your skillful implementation of these strategies is essential to your students' mastery of the CCSS or other rigorous standards, no matter the grade level or subject you are teaching. Other instructional strategies covered in the Essentials for Achieving Rigor series, such as analyzing errors in reasoning and engaging students in cognitively complex tasks, exemplify the cognitive complexity needed to meet rigorous standards. Taken as a package, these strategies may at first glance seem quite daunting. For this reason, the series focuses on just one strategy in each guide.

Processing New Information

The active cognitive processing of new information is an essential aspect of mastering critical content. This type of processing requires that students keep new information in their working memories for a sufficient period of time to act on it in a meaningful way before adding additional information. The visible manifestations of active processing include talking, sharing, explaining, writing, summarizing, paraphrasing, and questioning. To be sure, students can process new information independently, but processing in a cooperative dyad, triad, or group is more effective when a class is large and heterogeneous. Absent strategically planned opportunities for active processing that follow short, but information-packed, critical-input experiences, most novice learners will retain little from their first encounters with new information.

Information-input experiences can be oral presentations or explanations by the teacher, visual presentations in the form of various media, or written text contained in textbooks and resource materials. Whether new information is heard, viewed, or read, learners of all ages need ongoing opportunities to actively process it. If you want your students to understand and retain the critical information of your discipline, provide them with some type of processing experience after every chunk of new critical information they hear, see, or read. Depending on the difficulty of the information or how well students are progressing, a processing opportunity can be as brief as two to three minutes or as long as thirty minutes.

The Effective Implementation of Processing New Information

The effective implementation of processing new information often requires a readjustment in thinking about how students learn as well as renewed planning efforts to incorporate what students need into every lesson. Consider that a typical agenda in some upper elementary and secondary classrooms can look like this:

- The teacher talks, lectures, and explains new material. Sometimes the teacher shows a video and asks students to take notes while they watch.

- The teacher may pause every now and then during a lecture to ask questions of students but often ends up providing the answer when students stare blankly or avoid eye contact.

- Sometimes with five minutes remaining in the class, the teacher gives a homework assignment to students—for example, "Complete this graphic organizer, write a short summary, or write a letter to your senator about your opinion on this issue."

- The bell rings and the students rush out into the hallway, unlikely to retain much of what happened during the class period.

In contrast, consider a scenario in a high school biology class where the teacher spends only ten to fifteen minutes on one topic before shifting to a processing activity. The teacher specifically builds in several different ways for students to process the same information. For example, when learning DNA structure, students construct a model of DNA from pipe cleaners. They then color a DNA diagram using the color scheme found on their pipe cleaner model. At some point, the teacher shows an overhead of the DNA structure and introduces another way to process the information (adapted from McEwan, 2007).

In most lower elementary grades, there are often more interactive opportunities for students to work with one another. However, even in these classrooms, there are still some teachers who maintain a tight grip on student learning, seldom releasing control to guide students to self-management. Students seldom have ongoing opportunities to learn cooperatively or actively process new learning. These teachers are the nonexamples of facilitating active processing of new information. Their classrooms are eerily silent absent the buzz of active processing.

Compare that scenario to a primary classroom in which the teacher teaches and models the use of a collaborative processing activity during which students are processing new vocabulary. Students have opportunities to read, write, and talk about the new words with a partner, processing new words and their meanings collaboratively, and the teacher intentionally involves every student in the learning. Once the partners get going in their animated back-and-forth conversations about new words and where they have previously encountered them at school or home, there is an excited hum in the classroom. It is the sound of active processing (adapted from McEwan & Bresnahan, 2008).

Wherever your instructional style falls on the continuum illustrated by these two sets of example/nonexamples, your students' understanding and retention will deepen if you intentionally plan for multiple ongoing opportunities for the active processing of new information using the instructional sequence found in Table 2.

Table 2: Using Active Processing to Acquire New Information

Lesson Segment	Learning Sequence
Part 1	The teacher begins a new unit of information with a preview activity and follows that with an initial presentation of a chunk of critical information. This part of the lesson takes about ten to twelve minutes.
Part 2	After presenting a "chunk," the teacher stops to give students a task to do with a partner or group to actively process the new information. The techniques in this guide will give you many ways to engage your students in this kind of cognitive processing.
Part 3	Following the processing, the teacher "presents" another chunk of new information. This chunk could be in the form of a brief video clip, or it could involve students reading a short section of text pertinent to the critical information with a partner. In either case, students have specific kinds of processing in which they will engage once each information-input segment has occurred.
Part 4	The teacher repeats the above cycle until all of the chunks of critical information for a lesson or unit have been introduced and processed.
Part 5	The teacher directs students to review the critical information chunks from the day and think about whether anything they learned in a previous lesson connects with their new learning. The teacher then asks them to engage in some kind of summarizing activity to connect the various information chunks.

The following teaching behaviors are associated with facilitating the active processing of new information:

- teaching and modeling various techniques for processing new information prior to their implementation

- planning and providing multiple opportunities for students to actively process new information during a unit of instruction

- organizing collaborative dyads, triads, and other types of groups to actively process new information

- facilitating the efficient and effective implementation of collaborative groups during the implementation of active processing

- encouraging and motivating students to persevere through the processing of challenging new information

- gradually releasing responsibility to students for their own active processing

- ongoing monitoring for the desired results of active processing

There are several common mistakes the teacher can make while seeking to become skilled at implementing this instructional strategy:

- The teacher fails to intentionally plan for an adequate amount and quality of opportunities for the active processing of new information.

- The teacher fails to appropriately use the power of collaborative groups to assist students in actively processing new information.

- The teacher fails to gradually release the reins of responsibility for learning to students.

Failing to Intentionally Plan for an Adequate Amount and Quality of Processing

Most teachers provide a few opportunities for active processing of new information, but to intentionally plan the quantity and quality of this kind of processing often requires rethinking how you plan and organize your lessons. There are many informal and quick ways you can facilitate the active processing of new information that do not take extensive forethought and planning. However, keep in mind that the benefits of this instructional strategy can only be realized for your students if you intentionally plan for adequate amounts of processing and vary the techniques you use to facilitate that processing.

Failing to Effectively Harness the Power of Collaborative Processing

Most students learn best when working in well-organized and monitored peer groups because they can draw upon their partners' experiences to enrich their personal experience with the information. Group processing supports active thinking because it provides additional opportunities for students to rehearse critical information. However, merely providing adequate time for group processing is not enough. As with all instructional strategies, teaching and modeling for students how to work in collaborative processing groups is essential to success.

Failing to Release Responsibility to Students

In the pressure-packed school day with its constant demands, you can easily lose your focus—racing through information to "cover" it and taking all of the responsibility on yourself for processing, thinking, and learning new information. At the end of an exhausting day, your students have not wrestled with complex information, engaged in the active processing of new learning, or experienced the frustration that is necessarily an aspect of mastering a difficult discipline, and *you* are exhausted. Gradually turn over the responsibility for thinking and learning to your students. You are responsible for direct and guided instruction. You are responsible for modeling and guiding independent practice. You are responsible for the facilitation of collaborative groups. Your students are responsible for demonstrating their learning in collaborative and independent ways—applying their learning.

Monitoring for the Desired Result

Here are the main sources of evidence that show you your students are able to actively process new information:

1. Students can explain or paraphrase what they have just heard.

2. Students volunteer predictions about new information.

3. Students voluntarily ask clarification questions about new information.

4. Students actively discuss new information by asking and answering questions.

5. Students generate conclusions about new information.

6. Students verbally summarize new information.

7. Students can write in response to new information.

Each technique in this book also has examples of monitoring specific to that technique.

Scaffolding and Extending Instruction to Meet Students' Needs

As you monitor for the desired result of each technique, you will likely realize that some students are not able to readily process new information.

Within each technique that is described in this guide, there are examples of ways to scaffold and extend instruction to meet the needs of your students. *Scaffolding* provides support that targets cognitive complexity, student autonomy, and rigor. *Extending* moves students who have already demonstrated the desired result to a higher level of understanding. These examples are provided as suggestions, and you should adapt them to target the specific needs of your students. Use the scaffolding examples to spark ideas as you plan to meet the needs of your English language learners, students who receive special education or lack support, or simply the student who was absent the day before. The extension activities can help you plan for students in your gifted and talented program or those with a keen interest in the subject matter you are teaching.

Teacher Self-Reflection

As you develop expertise in teaching students to process new information, reflecting on your skill level and effectiveness can help you become more successful in implementing this strategy. Use the following set of reflection questions to guide you. The questions begin simply, with reflecting on how to start the implementation process, and move to progressively more complex ways of helping students process new information.

1. How can you begin to incorporate some aspect of this strategy into your instruction?

2. How can you engage student groups in processing new information?

3. How can you monitor the extent to which active processing increases students' understanding?

4. How might you adapt and create new techniques for processing of new information that address unique student needs and situations?

5. What are you learning about your students as you adapt and create new techniques?

Instructional Techniques to Help Students Process New Information

There are many ways to facilitate the processing of new information by your students. These ways or options are called *instructional techniques*. The instructional techniques you choose will depend on your grade level and content. The purpose of every technique in this guide is to enable you to facilitate opportunities for your students to "chew and digest" specific small chunks of curricular information. The digestive metaphor is an apt one. Expecting students to assimilate large units of complex information without regular breaks to cognitively process the new material will lead to certain cognitive overload for most, if not all, of your students.

In the following pages, you will find descriptions of how to implement the following techniques:

- Instructional Technique 1: Using Collaborative Processing

- Instructional Technique 2: Using Think-Pair-Share

- Instructional Technique 3: Using Concept Attainment

- Instructional Technique 4: Using Jigsaw

- Instructional Technique 5: Using Reciprocal Teaching

- Instructional Technique 6: Using Scripted Cooperative Dyads

All of the techniques are similarly organized and include the following components:

- a brief introduction to the technique

- ways to effectively implement the technique

- common mistakes to avoid as you implement the technique

- examples and nonexamples from elementary and secondary classrooms using selected learning targets or standards

- ways to monitor for the desired result

- ways to scaffold and extend instruction to meet the needs of students

Instructional Technique 1

USING COLLABORATIVE PROCESSING

Cooperative learning by definition is a teaching model in which students work in groups to accomplish tasks or projects the teacher assigns. The effects of a rigorous implementation of cooperative learning on student achievement can be seen in a solid body of research (Johnson et al., 1981; Walberg, 1999). The cooperative model is an indispensable tool in facilitating your students' active processing of new information. Cooperative learning differs from simple group work in two important ways: 1) individual and group accountability are built into every processing activity so that all group members are required to participate and produce *and* 2) group members are taught and then expected to fulfill certain roles during the cooperative process (McEwan, 2007). You cannot assume that your students will understand these two essential aspects of cooperative learning merely because they have "used it" in other classrooms. Take time at the beginning of each school year or new semester to model and directly teach your students how active processing works using the cooperative model. Heterogeneous cooperative groups provide all students with a measure of control over their own learning and provide struggling students with opportunities to work with strong academic role models.

How to Effectively Implement Processing New Information Using Collaborative Approaches

The effective implementation of processing new information using collaborative techniques requires that you take a careful look at exactly how you view the widely used teaching model known as cooperative learning. There is no real difference between the dictionary definitions of the terms *cooperative* and *collaborative*—they both suggest a shared effort to accomplish a task or endeavor. They also appear as synonyms for each other in the thesaurus. In some contexts, authors refer to students working together as cooperative and teachers working together as collaborative. In this technique, as in other techniques found in the book, the term *collaboration* has a more nuanced meaning that conveys what happens when students and teachers are working together to extract and construct multiple meanings from presentations, conversations, discussion, and the reading together of texts. Grouping students in dyads and triads only increases the opportunities students have to actively process new information.

Whether you love the cooperative learning model or feel it just does not fit your instructional style, consider harnessing the power of collaborative processing to enable your students to actively process new information.

Collaborative processing groups provide many ways for students to become more engaged and successful learners: 1) learning with peers provides students with multiple reference points for understanding new information; 2) students can observe how others process information and pick up practices to use in their own thinking; 3) students can acquire new perspectives regarding the information; 4) students can receive feedback from peers as they make their own thinking available to their peer group; and 5) students have daily opportunities to immediately try out and rehearse new information while it is still fresh in their working memories (adapted from Marzano, 2007).

There are two perspectives to consider prior to implementing the processing of new information using collaborative processing with your students: 1) directly teaching your students the what, why, when, and how of collaborating to process new critical content; and 2) acquiring some new teaching behaviors that are essential for the effective implementation of this technique.

Teach Your Students the What, Why, When, and How of Collaboration

Teaching your students how to engage with peers—the purpose of working together with a partner or a small group—and giving them clear explanations and directions relative to what they should share are prerequisites to processing new information using collaborative processing. For example, the mere act of students sharing with a partner absent a clear understanding of *how* the information is to be shared, *why* the sharing is taking place at this particular moment in time, and *what* exactly is to be shared can often be a waste of time. The desired result of all the collaborative techniques you will find in the pages ahead is that your students will have processed new information in a meaningful way toward the ultimate goal of acquiring long-lasting and meaningful learning. Table 1.1 presents a brief summary of the what, why, when, and how of collaborative processing that you can adapt for your grade level.

Table 1.1: The What, Why, When, and How of Collaborative Processing

The Question	The Answer
What is collaborative processing?	Collaborative processing is a way of organizing students for learning. It is not the only way students can learn. Effective teachers use other models to vary each class period and make various aspects of learning more motivating.
Why do we use collaborative processing in our classroom?	We use collaborative processing because students are more likely to understand and retain new information when they have opportunities to process that information with their peers. Collaborative processing gives students other perspectives on information in addition to the teacher's ideas. It teaches them to depend on others to accomplish some learning tasks.
When do we use collaborative processing in our classroom?	We use collaborative processing when we are introduced to new information that is often difficult to understand and remember. We use collaborative processing to talk, think, write, question, summarize, and generalize about new content. Collaborative processing increases the learning potential of every student.
How does collaborative processing work?	Social psychologists developed collaborative processing to harness the power of relationships between teachers and students to accomplish tasks and projects. However, educators who use this kind of processing in their classroom can point to benefits that go far beyond the social and emotional outcomes.

Incorporate Four Specific Teaching Behaviors for Effective Implementation

The cooperative learning model has been employed in classrooms for decades, often leading to feelings on the part of many educators that they already know all they need to be successful because they were the recipients of cooperative learning techniques in their own academic coursework, endure many more hours of these processes in professional development sessions, and always throw in a pair/share activity when a supervisor is observing them. However, there are four specific teaching behaviors that are essential for the successful implementation of collaborative processing: 1) explaining, 2) giving directions, 3) modeling, and 4) facilitating (McEwan-Adkins, 2010). These teaching behaviors can add value to all of the collaborative processing techniques you currently use in your classroom.

Explaining

Explaining involves providing students with verbal input about what will happen as they use a specific processing technique, what the goals are, why the students are using it, how it will help them, and precisely what the roles of the students and teachers will be as the students process new information. The sample below provides a brief snapshot of what explaining looks like in terms of collaborative processing.

A Sample Teacher Script for Explaining Collaborative Processing

Class, today we're going to begin learning about a classroom activity called collaborative processing. I know that many of your teachers have used similar activities, but I want to explain some important things you should know about collaborative processing. In this classroom, collaborative processing means that two or more students are talking together about something they have heard or read.

There are many ways to learn new things, and as the information in your textbooks becomes more complicated and important, I want to make sure that you have lots of opportunities to learn. Collaborative processing helps you understand and remember new and difficult information because you can talk about it with a partner and help each other understand.

When two or more students work together on learning new material, collaborative processing gives the team more learning power than if each person has processed the new information individually.

Giving Directions

Teachers gives hundreds of directives in the course of a day, sometimes not stopping to think about what may be going on in the minds of their students as they rush on to the next lesson. Giving directions involves providing unambiguous and concise verbal input that gives students a way to get from where they are at the beginning of a lesson, task, or unit to the achievement of a specific task or outcome. Giving directions should include more than just "teacher talk." It should provide wait time for students to process the directions, time for them to respond, and opportunities for them to ask clarifying questions. The sample on the next page shows an example of giving directions in the context of using collaborative processing.

A Sample Teacher Script for Giving Directions for Collaborative Processing

Class, right now, I am going to give you some directions for a new activity we will be using in our classroom called collaborative processing. I am going to write the steps you will follow on the chart paper and leave it up on the board.

1. Clear off your desk (table, work area) so your belongings won't distract you.

2. Find your partner, and together walk to the rug and sit down. If your partner is absent, I will find a new partner for you. I will be the partner of anyone who doesn't have a partner.

3. When you are sitting quietly on the rug next to your partner, give me the thumbs-up signal.

Modeling

Modeling is one of the most underappreciated and seldom used teaching behaviors in many classrooms. Teachers of music, art, physical education, science, and foreign language cannot teach their information without modeling. However, when critical information and cognitive processes are less visible and more cerebral, teachers suddenly fast-forward through the modeling step. That could be because modeling involves thinking aloud regarding your own cognitive processing, giving students an opportunity to gain a deeper understanding of what goes on in the brain of the teacher to accomplish something as mysterious as writing a summary, making a prediction, or drawing a conclusion. The breakdown occurs precisely at that point when the teacher has not really acquired the skill to write a summary or has not wrestled with exactly how many steps are involved in drawing a conclusion or asserting a claim. The following sample provides a brief snapshot of a teacher thinking aloud about how he writes a summary.

A Sample Teacher Script for Summarizing Using Collaborative Processing

Today, I want to model for you how I would write a summary of that first chunk of new information. I know that the first thing I have to do is make sure I really understand what I've read. If I feel a little shaky about understanding what I've read, I do two things. The first thing is I go back and read the chunk over again. I don't like to do that. I could be writing a fantastic summary while I'm reading the chunk again. It feels like a waste of time for me. So, I am always surprised by the fact that when I actually do read the chunk a second time, I now understand it better.

Rereading is one thing I do to help my comprehension. The second thing I do is see if there are any big words that I should look up in the glossary or on the internet for definitions. That will definitely help my comprehension.

So, after I've reread the text and found the meanings of words I didn't know, I'm ready to write my summary. Now, I'm going to show you the chunk of text that I'm supposed to be summarizing up on the screen. The next thing I do is figure out if there's anything in that chunk that isn't important. I know you're thinking everything is important. But, that's where authors fool you. Some things are more important than other things, and if you're summarizing, you not only have to figure out what's important, you also have to figure out what isn't important. I wonder about some authors when they include so much stuff that isn't important. Do they really know what is important?

Sometimes, to keep the unimportant stuff from distracting me, I cross it out. Now I reread what's left—the important stuff.

Then, I look for some key words and maybe some important details, and I usually just write those down so I won't forget them. The last thing I do is figure out a way to make a sentence out of those words I wrote down so I can tell the main idea in a few of my own words.

Now, you and your partner are going to be using these steps for summarizing when you work together. Remember that summarizing is always a challenge when you start doing it the first time. So, don't be discouraged. The more summaries you write, the easier the process will become.

Facilitating

Facilitating is the most essential behavior during the day-to-day implementation of collaborative processing. Without the ability to facilitate, your fallback positions as a teacher are telling and directing. Facilitating involves thinking along with students and helping them develop their own ideas, rather than managing their thinking by telling them what the text means and giving them ready-made answers to fill in the blanks of worksheets or notebooks. Facilitating is making the right things happen for students by talking to them and gradually releasing the responsibility for learning, thinking, and writing. Facilitation is an active, lively, and inquiring teaching behavior. Facilitators are listening to determine if students are heading in the right direction. When they are not, the facilitator asks questions to lead them down more productive paths. To effectively process new information using collaborative processing, the facilitating teacher is alert to those pairs or small groups whose sharing has nothing to do with the lesson. Perhaps the class needs a refresher regarding the purpose of the sharing. The following sample presents a brief classroom script showing facilitation in action.

A Sample Teacher Script for Facilitating During Collaborative Processing

Class, while you are working with your partners to summarize a new chunk of information, I'm going to check in with each pair to see how your collaborative processing is coming along.

To a pair of students who seem to be making no progress at all, the teacher asks, "So, what are you guys stuck on here?" They can't even articulate what's wrong. So, she continues to ask more questions: "Did you take turns reading the chunk sentence by sentence?" They both nod yes. "That's good," says the teacher. "Are there any big words that are confusing you?" They both shake their heads no. "So," says the teacher, "you just can't quite figure out how to get started. Remember when I modeled this process for the class, and I wrote my steps and tacked them on the board?" The boys look a little sheepish. "Well, OK then," the teacher says. "What do you think is the most important idea in this first chunk?" The boys brighten up. They know the answer. The teacher prompts them at a few more intervals, and they are on their way.

She stops to observe another pair of students. They are disagreeing about what the most important thing is in this chunk. The teacher doesn't tell them but asks some leading questions. The problem is that one student doesn't quite understand the difference between important and unimportant. The teacher provides an example from real life for the student. She asks her, "Do you have a dog?" The student nods yes. The teacher says, "What's the most important thing about your dog? You can pick only one thing." "But," the student says, "there are lots of important things about my dog."

"But," the teacher says, "one thing is more important than any of the other things. If you can't figure out what's important about your dog, how in the world can you figure out what's important in this chunk?" "Oh," says the student. "I have to pick just one thing?" "Yes," says the teacher. "Now give it a try."

Next, the teacher stops at the table of a pair of students who are obviously not collaborating toward the goal of writing a summary of the new information. They are talking about a friend who is in trouble with her parents. The teacher gives them a stern look and suggests that if they immediately get busy, they might just get out of class today without a write-up. If not, she will have them back here after school working on their summary before they go home.

Once you teach your students about collaborative processing and are more skilled in using the behaviors that make the technique run smoothly, try two techniques described in *The Art and Science of Teaching* (Marzano, 2007): one for processing new *declarative* information and a second for processing new *procedural* information. They are particularly useful for processing after small chunks of new information are presented.

In both of these techniques, the teacher organizes students into groups of three and designates each student in the group with the letter *A*, *B*, or *C*. As the teacher presents three segments of content, each student will have the opportunity to summarize and lead the discussion. After the first segment of content input, the teacher asks the students designated *A* in each group to briefly summarize the information. The other group members add additional information or bring up questions about things they do not understand. At this point, the teacher addresses any questions or confusion in the whole group before moving on and asks students to predict what they think the next chunk of new information will be about. Table 1.2 enumerates the steps for implementing the A-B-C Triad Technique.

Table 1.2: Implementing the A-B-C Triad for Processing New Information

Steps in the A-B-C Triad Collaborative Processing Technique	
1. Organize your students into groups of three, and ask the students in each group to label themselves A, B, or C.	
2. Explain the role that each student will play as leader of the group in summarizing and describing the new information the teacher will present. Explain the responsibilities of the other two group members: to add to what the leader says or identify aspects of the content that were confusing.	
3. Prepare a lesson containing three chunks of critical content. After you present the first chunk, direct the A students to act as group leaders to summarize the information. Remind the B and C students to add information or raise clarifying questions. Then ask the whole class whether they have any questions, and close out the first collaborative processing segment with students making predictions about what the next chunk will be about.	
4. Present the second chunk of new information, and repeat the process described in Step 3 with the B students serving as group leaders.	
5. Present the third chunk of new information, and repeat the process described in Step 3 with the C students serving as group leaders.	
Declarative Knowledge	Procedural Knowledge
If the new information you are presenting is declarative, such as that found in subjects with a great deal of critical content, this collaborative technique provides an efficient and positive way to actively process new information.	If the content you are presenting is procedural, such as writing or editing, or the execution of a particular move in a physical education class, the teacher will demonstrate one step of the process, and students will then rehearse it individually. Students can generate questions about their demonstration of the procedure similarly to questions asked about declarative knowledge.

Common Mistakes

The implementation of processing new information using collaborative processing techniques can often feel like a juggling act. There is so much to consider and so many ways to fail. However, do not become discouraged. Knowing in advance about the mistakes you might make usually lessens the odds that you will make them. Watch out for these common mistakes when you implement processing new information using collaborative processing:

- The teacher fails to explain the what, why, when, and how of collaborative processing.

- The teacher fails to model and teach the process to students before implementing it with new information.

- The teacher fails to allow time for students to practice the process with less-demanding content.

- The teacher fails to allow time for students to adequately process the new information before moving on to the next activity.

- The teacher fails to appropriately group students.

- The teacher fails to continuously facilitate and monitor collaborative processing.

Examples and Nonexamples of Processing New Information Using Collaborative Processing

Following are two examples (one elementary and one secondary) and their corresponding nonexamples of processing new information using collaborative processing. As you read, think about experiences you have had in your own classroom. Consider the common mistakes, and note how the example teachers cleverly avoid them and the nonexample teachers miss the mark by making one or more of the mistakes.

Elementary Example of Processing New Information Using Collaborative Processing

The learning target for this example is *read closely to determine what the text says explicitly* (CCR Anchor Standard 1 for Reading) *and to summarize the key supporting details and ideas* (CCR Anchor Standard 2 for Reading).

The fourth-grade teacher of our example class is frustrated by the haphazard reading habits her students have fallen into—habits that all too frequently lead to confusion rather than comprehension. She has developed a collaborative processing activity called Read-Decide-Explain (adapted from McEwan-Adkins & Burnett, 2012). She selects some short sections of text from recent units in the students' social studies and science textbooks. Although she has already "covered" the units in class, she is concerned that a great many of her students did not process the information adequately. She wants her students to read more carefully and pay more attention to what the text actually says. She begins with the first sample text titled "The Changing Earth" (McEwan, Dobberteen & Pearce, 2008) and divides it into three chunks. Here is how she explains the collaborative reading process to her students:

> Class, today we're going to work on a collaborative reading process called Read-Decide-Explain. You are going to work with a partner to read an article titled "The Changing Earth." The information should be familiar to you since we studied this unit several weeks ago. I am going to give you a question to answer. To find the answer, you are going to take turns reading this article aloud sentence by sentence with your partner. After reading each sentence in the chunk, you and your partner will decide whether the answer to the question I asked can be found in that sentence and then explain why or why not. Once you have completed a chunk, you and your partner are going to write a one-sentence summary of how the text in the chunk explicitly answers the question.

The teacher hands out two items, a copy of the article and a think sheet for students to record their answers, and says, "I'm going to model how this process works with a volunteer. Who would like to help me?" Henry raises his hand, and she asks him to come to the front. She displays the text on the screen and gives Henry a copy of the think sheet on which every sentence is numbered. Then she introduces the question she wants students to answer: "What does the text explicitly say caused the land surface of the earth to change? Explain your answer."

She points to the first sentence and asks Henry to read it aloud: "1) The land surface of the earth has not always looked as it does today."

She asks Henry to look at the think sheet, find the row for Chunk 1 / Sentence 1, and decide: "Does this sentence have anything to say that would help you answer the question? Yes or no, Henry."

Henry looks a little puzzled, and then his thinking skills kick in. "No," he answers.

The teacher directs him to write "No" in the Decide column. "Now, Henry, please explain your answer to us. Why did you say no? I'll give you some time to think about this."

The answer is not a difficult one, but most students are not accustomed to being held accountable this way. Henry finally comes through for the teacher and replies: "The sentence just tells what the topic is, but it doesn't tell anything about what caused the land surface to change."

"Terrific," says the teacher.

She explains that the pairs will work on the first chunk that contains three sentences, one of which has already been completed for them, and explains further: "Be sure to take turns reading the sentences aloud and answering the 'Decide' question. Then, the pairs will have to write a one-sentence summary of how the text in the chunk explicitly answers the question."

The teacher walks around the classroom listening to the discussions and watching students dig meaning out of text sentence by sentence. Her goal is that eventually students will assume the responsibility for this kind of careful reading.

The teacher looks upon this collaborative processing experience in which her students are engaging as an opportunity to help her students actively process new information on a regular basis without any scaffolds. If this experience is successful, she plans to implement it regularly when she introduces new information and wants her students to process the text themselves.

Elementary Nonexample of Collaborative Processing

The learning target for this elementary nonexample is *read closely to determine what the text says explicitly* (CCR Anchor Standard 1 for Reading), and summarize the key supporting details and ideas (CCR Anchor Standard 2 for Reading). The nonexample teacher is intrigued by the Read-Decide-Explain collaborative processing technique but feels that students have to learn to work independently when it comes to reading information text. She is willing to try the process on the recommendation of her colleague across the hall. She feels that reading something students have already read once will be boring for them, so she selects a more difficult text that contains a more challenging text structure and vocabulary level but is of high interest to them. She merely explains the process to her students without modeling at least a part of the process. Attempting to use a new technique with text that is more difficult to read results in a breakdown of the lesson. Students are unable to puzzle through the text while at the same time answering questions and writing summaries.

Secondary Example of Collaborative Processing

The learning target for this secondary example is *assess how point of view or purpose shapes the information and style of text* (CCR Anchor Standard 6 for Reading). The freshman English teacher is teaching her students how to identify the point of view of a specific piece of writing and decides to adapt a collaborative processing technique to motivate her students to actively process the information. She prepares a presentation on the topic on the standard (adapted from McEwan-Adkins & Burnett, 2012).

The presentation contains three chunks of information: 1) purpose—why the author is writing the text, 2) information—what the text is about, and 3) style—how the author uses language.

She selects an op-ed article from the local newspaper as the text that she and her students will use. She divides the text into three chunks. She presents the first chunk to students by describing a variety of questions they can "ask the author" while they are reading, explaining each one and then offering examples from texts they have read so far during the year. She stops and asks students to silently read the first chunk of the article and then talk with a partner about the purpose the author had in mind when writing the first chunk and to write the purpose(s) down on their think sheet. She now begins the second part of her presentation that explains how to determine the critical information in the text or what the text is about. Here is how she introduces this chunk of new information:

> Class, you did a great job figuring out the author's purpose in writing this first chunk of text. Now that we've identified the author's purpose in this first chunk, we're going to dig into the information in the same chunk and figure out what the text is mainly about (the central idea) and identify some of the key supporting details. Since you've already read the first chunk once, be thinking as I tell you about the different ways that authors make their information interesting to their readers.

The teacher goes on to describe the multiple ways that authors use the central idea and supporting details in their writing. She encourages students to think in terms of the first chunk and see if they can identify any of these ways in the text. She continues:

> I saw many of you nodding during my little presentation when you realized that the author of the text you are reading used several different ways to get across the central idea of the text. Working with your partner, identify as many of these ways as you can, and write them on your think sheet.

The partners are working together well, and there is an active hum of discussion about the article. The teacher calls time to remind them that she has one more brief presentation of information, this one on how the author uses language in unusual and interesting ways, which is his style. She introduces this final chunk:

> This last aspect of an author's writing is style: how the author uses language to make his writing style unique to him. *She explains each of the various aspects of style, some of which are new to students: diction, syntax, figurative language, imagery, and various sound devices. She says they may have to dig into that first chunk of text even more deeply to find examples of these, but the collaborative pairs are eager to give it a try.*

When they finish, the teacher asks students to write an individual summary statement that describes two things: 1) what they learned from the teacher and 2) what they learned while working with their partner. The teacher collects these as students exit class and is eager to read their "reviews" of this new collaborative processing experience.

Secondary Nonexample of Cooperative Learning

The learning target for this secondary example is *assess how point of view or purpose shapes the information and style of text* (CCR Anchor Standard 6 for Reading). The teacher would like to use a collaborative processing technique with his students but is reluctant to turn over so much of the responsibility of this important standard to them. He much prefers to take control of the process and lectures to his students on the purpose, information, and style as they take notes on an organizer he has prepared for them. He does stop every now and then to ask if students have any questions, but everyone is still busy writing, so he continues his lecture. Students have no opportunity to rehearse their new learning following the teacher's content input, and there is no peer from whom to gain another perspective on what can be a very challenging cognitive task: assessing how point of view or purpose shapes the information and style of text.

Determining If Students Can Process New Information Using Collaborative Processing

The ongoing interactions between and among students while they are collaboratively processing information demands that you be on high alert, monitoring your students for both their success in collaborating with each other and also the degree to which they are actively processing and understanding new content. To keep your fingers on the pulse of learning in your classroom requires that you assemble a tool kit of ways that you can monitor your students' understanding of new information acquired through collaborative processing. Here are ways to help you:

- Collect, before the students exit the classroom, summaries they wrote with their partners about each chunk of content you presented.

- Collect, before students exit the classroom, summaries that they independently wrote of the overall presentation.

- Listen and answer questions as students summarize and clarify content.

- Observe the ways in which students are using appropriate collaborative techniques as they work with their groups.

The student proficiency scale for processing new information using collaborative processing in Table 1.3 displays the range of student proficiencies for using collaborative techniques to process new information. Use the scale to reflect the precise ways you plan to identify the desired result of this technique.

Table 1.3: Student Proficiency Scale for Processing New Information Using Collaboration

Emerging	Fundamental	Desired Result
Students can identify new information.	Students summarize new information.	Students accurately summarize new information.
Students listen to other perspectives.	Students discuss their perspective.	Students actively discuss multiple perspectives, adding on to others' ideas.
	Students identify important aspects of new information.	Students explain and discuss important aspects of new information.

Scaffold and Extend Instruction to Meet Students' Needs

Many students will have difficulty processing new information for three primary reasons: 1) there is a lack of background knowledge, 2) the students have difficulty decoding and comprehending grade-level materials, and 3) the students need language and learning supports. Meeting the needs of this diverse group of students requires that you adapt your instruction.

Conversely, there will be students who may arrive in your class already knowing a great deal about the new content you propose to teach. They will also need some type of adaptation. Here are some ideas for developing scaffolds and extensions to meet students' needs:

Scaffolding

- Provide alternative resources based on students' reading levels.

- Provide resources in varying media—for example, audio or video clips.

- Group students with similar learning needs, and in the beginning, facilitate the group during the first few times they need to process new information in a collaborative setting.

Extending

- Have students develop multimedia resources for new content that other students can use in the classroom or at home.

- Have a pair of students plan a content-input segment in which they present new information to their classmates.

- Have students independently read more difficult books that enrich the new content.

Instructional Technique 2

PROCESSING NEW INFORMATION USING THINK-PAIR-SHARE

The most widely known and often used technique for processing new information using collaborative processing is called Think-Pair-Share (Lyman, 1981). The staying power of this process in classrooms at every level attests to its ease of use, effectiveness, and adaptability to almost any instructional setting. But the most important attribute of Think-Pair-Share is the way in which it virtually guarantees that every student participates in collaborative processing. When a group has more than two individuals, there is always the possibility that one member will choose to disengage from the process, or that two or more of the other members will form their own subgroup, effectively shutting out the others. Most teachers use Think-Pair-Share in professional development trainings, faculty meetings, and their own classrooms. However, the effective implementation of Think-Pair-Share involves the mastery of several important chunks of critical information: 1) the basic vocabulary of Think-Pair-Share, 2) the basic steps of Think-Pair-Share, 3) how to teach and model Think-Pair-Share, and 4) how to plan for Think-Pair-Share.

The Basic Vocabulary of Think-Pair-Share

The terms *think*, *pair*, and *share* have specific meanings in the context of the process. You might also choose to add the term *write* to the vocabulary you teach your students in advance of implementation. Table 2.1 displays student-friendly definitions of the Think-Pair-Share terms.

Table 2.1: Student-Friendly Definitions for Think-Pair-Share

Student-Friendly Definition of the Term	Explanatory Notes for the Teacher
Think: Concentrate on something to come up with an idea, understanding, or opinion about it.	You can adapt this definition so that it is more meaningful for your students. However, once you've presented the definition, use it whenever you are talking about the process.
Pair: Two of something; in the case of Think-Pair-Share, two students whom the teacher assigns to work with each other or who choose to work with each other on a project.	There are many ways to pair students for collaborative processing using the Think-Pair-Share technique. Share your favorite ways with colleagues, and borrow an idea or two from those who have been using this technique for many years.
Share: Tell somebody something about what you have learned from listening, reading, or viewing information about it.	In the context of Think-Pair-Share, sharing can be sharing with your partner, a second set of partners, or with the whole class.
Write: Put your thoughts into words on paper.	If you add writing to the Think-Pair-Share technique, it will extend the length of the lesson. However, when your information is cognitively complex, you may wish to have partners write something during the Pair phase, or you may choose to add a writing phase at the end of the lesson to ask students to individually summarize the important things they want to remember about the day's lesson.

The Basic Steps of Think-Pair-Share

There are two sets of lesson steps for the Think-Pair-Share method. The first lesson contains the steps Lyman (1981) originally developed. They are generic, and you can use them in almost any setting. They are enumerated in Table 2.2.

The second set of steps is specifically adapted for processing new information. Be clear that if you desire to process new information and help your students engage with critical information, you will want to use the lesson steps described in Table 2.3. Take a moment to compare the two sets of steps.

You will note the difference immediately. Lyman's original lesson is a self-contained unit in which the teacher uses the process more in the nature of an advanced organizer or as a way to activate prior knowledge. While these are certainly appropriate uses of this technique, the generic approach does not fulfill the processing needs you have during the presentation of critical information. At that point, you want a technique to facilitate the active processing of new information.

Table 2.2: Lesson Steps for Frank Lyman's Original Version of Think-Pair-Share

Lesson Step	Explanatory Notes for Teacher
1. Suggest a problem for the students to solve, or ask an open-ended question.	Endeavor to connect the problem or question to critical information.
2. Provide some time for students to engage in the first task: thinking about the problem or question.	In some cases, teachers provide a template or think sheet on which students can record the results of their thinking.
3. After an appropriate amount of think time, direct the students to turn to their partner to talk about the questions or problem (the pairing part of the process).	The length of time you devote to each of these aspects of the process will depend on your students and the complexity of the problem or question.
4. After the partners share, they can share with another set of partners or with the whole group, as you direct.	Drawing the Think-Pair-Share process to a productive conclusion takes practice. Do not have students lead you into a drawn-out sharing session that is not in your lesson plan.

Lesson steps are adapted from Lyman (1981). Explanatory notes for the teacher are original to the authors.

As previously noted, the set of steps in Table 2.3 are specifically adapted and modified from Lyman's work to enable you to help your students become more skilled at collaboratively processing new information using Think-Pair-Share.

Table 2.3: Lesson Steps for Processing New Information From a Teacher-Taught Lesson

Lesson Step	Explanatory Notes for the Teacher
1. Present a chunk of new information. Instruct students to listen for what is most important about the information you will share.	The most important thing about any lesson in which you plan to use Think-Pair-Share after each chunk of information input is making sure you identify the critical information in the content for your students, so when it is time for them to think, your input will provide lots of information for them to think about. If you do not specifically identify what it is you want your students to carry away from that ten-minute chunk of lesson, they will have nothing meaningful to process.
2. After the information presentation, ask students a question or suggest a thinking task related to the new information and give students time to think about it (not more than thirty seconds).	Lower elementary students can process small chunks in about thirty seconds. Older students will need more time since both the information and thinking task are likely to be more cognitively demanding.
3. Once the think time is over, direct students to get "knee to knee" and "eye to eye" with their partners so they can quietly exchange ideas, answer your question, or identify something they do not understand.	Pairing with a partner is difficult if partners are far away from one another. If you intend to use Think-Pair-Share frequently, arrange your desks, tables, and chairs in a way that facilitates collaborative processing.
4. You have three options: 1) resume the information input of another chunk of new information, 2) have the partners share ideas with another set of partners, or 3) have the partners share their ideas with the whole class.	Choose option 1 if you have two or more chunks of information left to present. Choose option 2 if you feel that additional processing is necessary for almost all students to feel confident about the new information. Choose option 3 to bring closure to a lesson and help students draw conclusions or summarize what they have learned.

Rasinski and Padak (2000) suggest the following adaptation (Table 2.4) of the Think-Pair-Share method for processing text after silent or choral reading.

Table 2.4: Processing New Information From a Short Text Selection

Lesson Step	Explanatory Notes for Teacher
1. Select sections of the textbook or other resource materials containing new critical information.	During your first implementation of this adaptation, choose text at a slightly easier reading level that still contains new critical information.
2. Chunk the information sections as appropriate to the text and the students' reading levels.	Based on your students' needs, decide whether to have students read silently or read chorally in pairs. The latter method ensures that a pair of students will finish the text at the same time and is a helpful way to scaffold a reader who may need support.
3. Direct students to read to the first stopping point.	At the first stopping point, your goal is to have students think about what they have read by actively processing new information from the text. You could use the same question or task after each chunk or facilitate this process by assigning a different task or question.
4. Direct the student pairs to share their ideas in response to your prompt or task.	You have two choices at this point: You could ask each pair to share with the whole class or gradually release the responsibility for processing the text to the students and not need to hear every single pair report.
5. The cycle begins again and continues until students read and process all chunks of text.	Keep the process moving along so as to maintain student engagement.

Lesson steps adapted from Rasinski & Padak (2000). Explanatory notes for the teacher are original to the authors.

How to Teach and Model Think-Pair-Share

One important part of the effective implementation of Think-Pair-Share is teaching and modeling the process to students. Table 2.5 contains a sample lesson in which a lower elementary teacher is teaching and modeling the Think-Pair-Share method. If you teach older students, you might conclude that this kind of modeling is not necessary for them. However, all students will benefit from appropriate direct teaching and modeling for any technique that you are using with them for the first time.

**Table 2.5: How to Teach and Model Think-Pair-Share
to Lower Elementary Students**

Lesson Objective	Students Are Able to Execute a Cooperative Learning Process Independently
Advance organizer	Teacher says: "Class, today we're going to learn how to work together as partners. When two people work together, they can learn new information more easily. The process is called Think-Pair-Share."
Teacher modeling	Teacher says: "Let me show you what each of these words look like, so you can get ready to Think-Pair-Share.
	When I *think*, I am using my brain to come up with an idea or answer. When I'm talking, I can't really be thinking at the same time. So when I'm thinking, my lips are sealed, and I have my thinking cap on. That's when I can get a really good idea." The teacher stops for a moment and adopts a thinking pose for a few seconds. "Sometimes it takes me longer to think of something interesting about what I have just heard.
	Just now, I had a very interesting thought about sunshine and how wonderful it would be if all the warmth from the sunshine could be stored and saved until the wintertime, when it gets cold. But, that's not what I am supposed to be thinking about. I need to think about what the teacher said or what I read.
	Now, the word *pair* means two things that go together. For this process, the 'pair' is a pair of students. Or, it could be one teacher and one student—a pair of learners. Jamie and Olive, stand up. Now I have a pair with one boy and one girl. Olive, please stand with me. Now it's a pair with one teacher and one student. Notice that when we're working in class, a pair always has two people in it.
	The third word is *share*. When I talk about sharing something with a friend, you might think of giving someone part of your lunch or sharing a game. The kind of sharing that you will be doing with this activity is sharing the ideas you came up with when you were thinking. Let me show what it looks like when two people share their ideas."

Single-student modeling	Teacher says: "Who has a good idea they could share with me about how the cafeteria could improve the lunches?" The teacher waits and then asks for a volunteer. The student comes to the front of the class, and the teacher models sitting down in her chair while facing the student, who is sitting in another chair.
	The student shares his idea with the teacher while she listens, quietly looking at the student in an attentive way. "Thank you, Sam, for sharing that idea with me. Now it's my turn to share my idea." The teacher gives her thoughts that the teacher's lunchroom should have soft-serve ice cream.
	She reminds students that when Sam was talking, she was listening. Then something that Sam said made her think of a good idea. She points out to students that she did not interrupt Sam, but waited until he finished.
Multi-student modeling	The teacher asks for another student volunteer, and they model talking to each other about another topic.
Peer demonstration using Think-Pair-Share	The teacher asks for two student volunteers to Think-Pair-Share at the front of the class.
Whole-class modeling using Think-Pair-Share	Teacher says: "Now we are going to Think-Pair-Share about reading. I would like all of you to think about one thing you do that helps you understand what you have read. Give me a thumbs-up when you are ready with your idea. When I see someone else with a thumbs-up, I'm going to give permission to that person to walk from her desk to pair with someone else who has a thumbs-up. That pair of students can get into line for recess and talk to each other in line."
	The teacher continues to pair up students and walk up and down the line that is forming, listening to the various suggestions. When most students are in line, the teacher uses the last five minutes for some sharing: "If your partner told you a good idea about reading, I want you to share it with the whole group."
Collaborative-effort modeling	The teacher continues to ask for more sharing until the recess bell rings.
Partnering using Think-Pair-Share	After recess, the teacher presents a math lesson and uses the Think-Pair-Share method for students to process new information about subtraction.

Plan for the Effective Implementation of Think-Pair-Share

There are three critical to-do items to include in your plan book whenever you use the Think-Pair-Share method to facilitate the active processing of new information: 1) build in adequate processing time, 2) identify and record the processing tasks you want students to think or write about, and 3) identify and note how you plan to monitor whether your students are achieving the desired effect of processing new information using the Think-Pair-Share technique.

Build in Adequate Processing Time

Make sure to intentionally plan for the allotted time needed for each instance in which you expect students to engage in the Think-Pair-Share process. Research shows that the quality of students' responses goes up significantly when you give them adequate think time. During the Think portion of this technique, students need time to think about what they have just heard or read and possibly retrieve any prior knowledge that may connect to the new knowledge, before they are prepared to turn to their partner and share.

Identify and Record the Questions or Tasks You Want Students to Think About and Share With Their Partners

To maximize the desired effects of using Think-Pair-Share to process new information that your students have either heard from you, seen in some type of visual format, or read in their textbooks or resource materials, develop the questions or tasks you wish to use at the same time that you select the various chunks of critical information. Remember that the reason for stopping after an information-input segment is to give your students opportunities to cognitively process the new information. Your question or task should be closely related to the information you presented. That way, students who were paying attention will have little difficulty thinking about how to respond to the questions or task and then sharing their ideas or answers with a partner.

Table 2.6 illustrates some types of questions you might ask your students. You want the conversations to be meaningful and rich. However, many Think-Pair-Share conversations are often off topic and time wasters because the questions and tasks the teacher presents are irrelevant and unrelated to critical content. Once students become accustomed to the process, vary the types of tasks you ask students to work on during the think time. Students could write, draw, or create their own questions during this time. During the Share time, students could write their responses on a whiteboard and share them with the class.

Table 2.6: Sample Sentence Starters and Questions for Using Think-Pair-Share

Sentence Starters	Questions
• What is the difference between _____ and _____?	• How would our country be different today if we had not elected Abraham Lincoln as president?
• What are the steps needed to solve for _____?	• Given Dwight Eisenhower's approach to economics, what could have been done differently to produce a better result?
• Reword the summary in your own words.	• We've been examining how the invention of fiber optics had an impact on communication. Describe a current event that historians of the future might conclude made a similarly profound impact on society. Justify.
• How have you seen this in your life?	
• What could be the definition for the word _____?	
• Write down all the things you remember about _____.	• We have just reviewed the steps of the scientific method. What do you think will happen after scientists share or publish the results of their experiments?
• Why do you think the author did _____?	
• Read and paraphrase.	
• What if _____?	
• How could we apply this idea today?	
• What do you think will happen next?	
• Write what you are unclear about.	

Note in Your Plan Book How You Plan to Monitor If Students Are Achieving the Desired Effect of the Technique

Actively monitor to ensure that your students' conversations are relevant and each of the partners in a pair has an equal opportunity to participate. Based on your monitoring, you may decide to provide additional support to some partnerships or rearrange some partner pairs. As you become more skilled in using this technique, you may be able to create monitoring opportunities more spontaneously. However, making the monitoring decision in advance will keep you and your students focused on your goal for the session. In addition to monitoring for the overall desired effect, ensure that students are ready to proceed to the next step of the technique. For instance, before moving along to the Pair phase of the process, ask students to give a thumbs-up or other indication to show when they are ready to move to the next phase.

Common Mistakes

There may be instances when problems arise during your implementation of processing new information using the Think-Pair-Share method. Knowing in advance where the roadblocks lie can result in a more effective implementation. Here are some common mistakes to avoid:

- The teacher fails to teach and model the technique for students.

- The teacher fails to provide the necessary think time and thereby undermines the effectiveness of the technique.

- The teacher fails to monitor students' processing to determine whether they are actively processing the new information that the teacher presents or the students read.

- The teacher fails to keep the process moving along in a timely fashion, and students' attention lags.

- The teacher fails to design questions and tasks for students to think about that are directly related to the new critical information.

- The teacher overuses the Think-Pair-Share method for unimportant or trivial tasks rather than focusing on students' active processing of critical information.

Examples and Nonexamples of Processing New Information Using Think-Pair-Share in the Classroom

Review the following examples and nonexamples from both elementary and secondary levels. Although the grade levels or information may differ from who and what you teach, use this opportunity to think about how you would design similar Think-Pair-Share opportunities for your students to process new information.

Elementary Example of Processing New
Information Using Think-Pair-Share

The learning target for this elementary example is *write narratives to develop real or imagined experiences or events using effective techniques, descriptive details, and clear event sequences* (CCSS.ELA-Literacy.W.4.3).

> Good morning, class. Today you are going to begin learning how to write a narrative. To help you understand and remember important information about narratives, we're going to use the Think-Pair-Share process. We've used this process in the past, and I'll review the instructions before we begin the process. But first, I want to tell you some important information about a kind of writing: a narrative. So listen intently for the important information about narratives.
>
> A *narrative* is a story. A narrative can be an imaginary story that you make up, or a narrative can be a story about something that has really happened to you. For example, if I wrote a story about a ten-year-old boy and his experiences growing up, that would be a narrative about an *imagined* experience. If I wrote a story about something that happened to me when I was a girl growing up, that would be a *real* experience. If I wrote an article about the various types of rocks, that would not be a narrative, because it isn't a story. If I wrote a story about going rock hunting on my vacation, that would be a narrative, and it would be true. But, if I wrote a story about an imaginary scientist and his adventures hunting for rocks in faraway places, that would be an imagined narrative.

The teacher has developed a think sheet for students to use during the Think aspect of the Think-Pair-Share and displays a copy of the template on her screen. Today, she asks them to process the new information she has presented about the two types of narratives that can be written and how they differ from one another. Here are the directions she gives to students about what they are to think (and write down) individually before they meet with their partners:

> First, listen carefully for what you need to think about and then write about on your think sheet. Think about what a narrative is, and decide what type of narrative you would like to write. Tell your partner why you made that choice. *This question requires that students understand what a narrative is, know that there are two types of narratives, and then make a choice to write one of the kinds and explain the reasons for doing so.*

In her second chunk of information input, the teacher continues to discuss the critical attributes of each type of narrative. As part of this chunk, she displays two short examples (one paragraph) of both kinds of narratives that she has prepared. They are similar to the examples she used in the first section of information input. She displays the examples on the screen and writes the attributes on each one as she presents them.

After turning off her projector, the teacher directs students to think and then write down as many critical attributes of the type of narrative they would like to write. She explains:

> If you told your partner earlier that you wanted to write a real story, write down several of the attributes or characteristics of that type of narrative. If you told your partner you wanted to write an imaginary story, write down those attributes. Now it's time to pair. If both partners are going to write the same type of narrative, I expect that they would have a nice long list of attributes. If each partner wants to write something different, help each other by remembering attributes of both kinds of narratives.

The teacher collects and reviews the students' think sheets and is pleased to find that they have been able to decide what kind of narrative they would like to write and list many different attributes. She will use this information to continue teaching the narrative the following day.

Elementary Nonexample of Processing New
Information Using Think-Pair-Share

The learning target for this elementary nonexample is *write narratives to develop real or imagined experiences or events using effective techniques, descriptive details, and clear event sequences* (CCSS.ELA-Literacy.W.4.3).

> Good morning, class. I want you to think about what you know about narratives. We just learned about this yesterday, and I'm giving you thirty seconds to jot down a list of the things you remember. I am setting my timer. Be ready . . . OK, time's up. Find two people to share your responses with. You have three minutes . . . OK, time's up. Go back to your seats, and be prepared to share your responses with the class. Remember, I will randomly call on students, so everyone should be prepared to discuss.

The teacher sets her timer to three minutes. When the timer rings, she calls on individual students to share their responses with the entire class.

The nonexample teacher makes a number of erroneous assumptions that undermine her efforts to effectively teach her students how to write narratives. She assumes that her students fully understand the purpose of the Think-Pair-Share process because they have used it in the past. She assumes that students are prepared to process new information from an earlier presentation, rather than presenting critical information and giving students immediate opportunities to actively process the information. She rushes the process and fails to monitor whether her students are achieving the desired effect of the process.

Secondary Example of Processing New Information
Using the Think-Pair-Share Method

The learning target for this secondary example is *solve systems of linear equations exactly and approximately* (CCSS.Math-Algebra.REI.6). A middle school algebra teacher posts a reminder on his class door: "Retrieve your content vocabulary notebook from the storage bin, and turn to the definitions and examples from last week." He opens his lesson by reviewing prior learning with his students:

Class, take a moment to review some very important learning from the past couple of weeks. You know what a *variable* is *[points to the definition on the Word Wall]*. You know what an *equation* is *[points to that definition on the Word Wall]*. You know the difference between a linear equation (one that graphs as a straight line) and a nonlinear equation.

Today, we are going to learn how to solve a system of linear equations. You have already learned how to solve a simple equation. A linear system of equations is one with two or more linear equations and two or more variables. We are going to solve a simple linear equation with two equations and two variables.

Some of you have told me that you are frustrated by all of the letters and numbers and signs you find in equations, and you've also asked me if algebra ever solves real problems. So, today, we are going to work with a real problem. Well, at least our problem has real stuff in it: a puppy and a kitten. As we move through the lesson, I'll stop every few minutes to give you a chance to talk to your partner. This opportunity to talk to someone else about what you heard me say will help you fix the new knowledge in your brain. So, the harder you think, pair, and share in the next hour, the less time you will have to spend on your homework or calling the tutor on the homework hotline. I guarantee it.

We've used Think-Pair-Share before. If the steps are fuzzy in your mind, look at the poster to remind yourself what you are supposed to do for each step. We're going to start out slow and then pick up speed, so stay with me. *The teacher puts the following word problem up on the screen: "A puppy weighs 16 pounds. When a kitten sits on the scale with the puppy, the combined weight of the animals is 26 pounds. How much does the kitten weigh?"*

Now, don't tell me how much the kitten weighs. I want to see the equation you wrote to solve this problem and a description that tells me what your solution means. Get ready to think and pair. Remember, one whiteboard per pair of students. If you and your partner agree on the answer, write it on the whiteboard, and hold it up to share it with the class.

The teacher is pleased to see that almost every pair of students has generated an appropriate equation ($16 + k = 26$) and the accurate description: k *is the weight of the kitten in pounds.* At the next opportunity for students to pair and talk about the critical information, the teacher makes a mental note to pay close attention to the three pairs of students who either could not agree regarding what to write on their whiteboards or wrote an incorrect answer. He notices that in one case, one of the pairs knew the answer immediately and insisted that they write the answer on the whiteboard rather than the equation and a description of the solved variable. The teacher quiets the students and moves on to the next chunk of information input. He puts up a new word problem on the screen: "The combined weight of a puppy and a kitten is 180 pounds. The sum of 3 times the weight of the puppy and twice the weight of the kitten is 414 pounds. Find the weight of each animal."

The teacher explains:

This word problem requires a system of linear equations. To answer the problem, you need to create two equations and find the values of two variables. Notice that the pets in this example have gained quite a bit of weight! I'm going to create the first equation for you—the easy one. Remember that we are designating the two variables *p* for puppy and *k* for kitten. The word problem tells us that the combined weight—that is, the weight of the two animals together—is 180 pounds. Just visualize this problem for a minute. We have a scale (it would have to be a bit larger than the average bathroom scale to weigh these two animals, because together they weigh 180 pounds). So, our equation is puppy (*p*) + kitten (*k*) = 180 pounds. We obviously can't solve this equation without taking the second step of creating another equation using the information in the word problem.

The teacher stops at this point and tells his students that it is time to Think-Pair-Share.

Think about the words in the problem, and follow those words to generate a second equation. When you create your second equation, write it on one whiteboard and get ready to share it with the class. I don't want you to solve this linear system just yet. We'll learn more about how to do that tomorrow.

The discussion between partners takes longer this time as students work to generate a second equation, but with his guidance and coaching, every pair of students writes an accurate representation of the word problem on a whiteboard. However, the teacher knows that his students often need word problem examples to bring more meaning into their algebra learning. During the whole-class sharing of the equations, the teacher encourages students to ask questions about any aspect of the critical information and engages them in one last Think-Pair-Share.

Here are the directions for your exit ticket for today: Divide one sheet of notebook paper into four equal parts. In the top left-hand square, write the first equation. In the top right-hand square, write the equation using words from the word problem. Notice that I have given you a good-bye gift today: I've completed the top half of your exit ticket for you. If you want to be ambitious and solve this system of linear equations before tomorrow, I will give you a "get-out-of-homework pass" good for any day of the week until winter break.

Students use the final ten minutes of the class period to think about and complete their exit ticket (Figure 2.1). The teacher collects them at the door, pleased that his students have actively processed his introduction to new information. He is even more pleased when two students arrive in class the next day with the solution: the puppy weighs 54 pounds, and the kitten weighs 126 pounds. Obviously, this kitten will be growing into a very large cat. One student has used the substitution method to solve this linear system, and the second student used the elimination method.

Figure 2.1: Sample Exit Ticket

Equation 1 $p + k = 180$	**Using Words From the Problem** The puppy's weight, p, plus the kitten's weight, k, is 180. or The puppy and the kitten together weigh 180 pounds.
Equation 2 $3p + 2k = 414$	**Using Words From the Problem** The sum (total) of 3 times the weight of the puppy and twice the weight of the kitten is 414 pounds.

The problems used in the secondary example are adapted from Ledwith (2014).

Secondary Nonexample of Processing New Information Using Think-Pair-Share

The learning target for the secondary nonexample is *solve systems of linear equations exactly and approximately* (CCSS.Math-Algebra.REI.6).

Our nonexample teacher is using the Think-Pair-Share method for the first time in her class. She decides to take a shortcut when it comes to teaching and modeling the process for her students and relies on the fact that most of her colleagues in the lower grades use the strategy so students are very familiar with the way it works. Once she arrives at the point in her lesson when it is time for students to do some thinking and then pair off with a partner, she looks at the clock and realizes that she does not have the time she needs to execute the process before the bell rings. So, she creates a new version of the process, called Think-Write, and assigns her students to solve the problem she has used in her presentation and hand it in as they leave the classroom. Balancing the complexity of the curriculum with the presentation and facilitation skills needed to implement various versions of Think-Pair-Share takes careful planning.

Determining If Students Can Process New Information Using Think-Pair-Share

Monitoring to determine if your students are actively processing new information using the Think-Pair-Share technique has two components: 1) looking for something that students do to demonstrate the desired result of the technique and 2) checking for the desired result and responding to students' progress. Here are some specific examples of monitoring while students are using Think-Pair-Share:

- The teacher moves around the classroom and listens to the students sharing their summary or paraphrase of the critical information to ensure they have processed the new information.

- The teacher listens for the students' accuracy and understanding of the new information about which they drew a conclusion based on their cognitive processing during the Think stage.

- The teacher makes sure that each student hands in an exit ticket demonstrating his thinking and sharing.

The student proficiency scale for processing new information using Think-Pair-Share is shown in Table 2.7. Use the scale to reflect the precise ways you plan to identify the desired result of this technique with your students.

Table 2.7: Proficiency Scale for Processing New Information Using Think-Pair-Share

Emerging	Fundamental	Desired Result
Students state what they have learned.	Students describe what they have learned.	Students can state multiple aspects of what they have learned.
Students use academic language in their paired discussions.	Students discuss important information in the chunk of content.	Students discuss their perspective about the important information in the chunk of content.
Students can create simple summaries or conclusions.	Students' summaries and conclusions contain the important information.	Students' summaries and conclusions include multiple perspectives.

Scaffold and Extend Instruction to Meet Students' Needs

Meeting the needs of the range of students in your classroom will likely require adapting the Think-Pair-Share technique through scaffolding the process for students who are struggling or extending instruction for students who are eager and able to move to a new challenge.

Scaffolding

- Create a poster of the technique, and illustrate it with visual cues.

- Provide additional processing time for students to think.

- Allow students to write their thoughts during the Think stage.

- Provide a question stem to students who may need assistance to think about the question or problem.

- Provide alternative resources based on students' reading levels.

- Provide resources in varying media—for example, audio or video clips.

- Use pictures or images as an alternative to a verbal prompt for students to ponder during the Think stage.

- Group students with similar learning needs, and remain with the group during the Pair stage.

Extending

Extending learning for accelerated or advanced students may include:

- Have a pair or foursome of students create a graphic representation of their summary or conclusion.

- Have a pair or foursome of students create a tech-savvy representation of their summary or conclusion—for example, an animation, a video, or a tweet.

Instructional Technique 3

USING CONCEPT ATTAINMENT

Concept attainment is a technique that "leads students to a concept by asking them to compare and contrast examples (called exemplars) that contain the characteristics (called attributes) of the concept with examples that do not contain those attributes" (Joyce & Weil, 1986, p. 27). Using this technique, you provide your students with specifics, and they must generalize from those examples, pulling together a complete and accurate picture of the concept you want them to master. The technique can be used at any grade level and for any type of information, but it is particularly suited to lessons in which you are introducing a complex concept that is central to a new unit of content. You will find several versions of the technique in addition to a popular game called Ins and Outs in this chapter.

How to Effectively Implement Concept Attainment

For students to become engaged in concept attainment, you and they must master the meanings of the following terms: *concept, example, nonexample, attribute, defining attribute*, and *nondefining attribute*. The terms are defined in Table 3.1.

Table 3.1: Definitions of Terms for Implementing Concept Attainment

Term	Definition and Discussion for the Teacher
Concept	An important idea related to your information. You might even call it a big idea. Choose the concepts for using concept attainment with care, making sure they are connected to your learning targets and are worthy of the time that you and your students will devote to them.
Example	An effective model of a specific concept.
Nonexample	An ineffective model of a specific concept.
Attribute	An attribute is a characteristic, trait, quality, or feature of a particular person, place, thing, or idea.
Defining attribute	A characteristic that must be present to distinguish a particular person, place, thing, or idea. For example, the defining attributes of triangles are that they are closed and three-sided.
Nondefining attribute	A nondistinguishing characteristic of a particular person, place, thing, or idea. For example, a triangle might have a different size, color, or orientation, but none of these attributes define a triangle.

There are two versions of the concept attainment technique. In the first version, a less demanding cognitive exercise, the teacher identifies the concept, a familiar one to students, and they then determine the attributes of that concept. This first version is more suited to younger students or for your first experience using the concept attainment technique as a teacher.

In the second, more demanding version of the technique, the teacher does not name the concept, often introducing it as a mystery term, and the students must make informed guesses about the concept based on the examples and nonexamples the teacher provides. A step-by-step lesson plan for introducing the first version to your students is shown in Table 3.2. Column 1 contains directions for the lesson step, while Column 2 provides additional explanatory information. Once you have read and understood Column 2, you need to consult Column 1 only when you wish to review the lesson steps.

Table 3.2: Teacher Names the Concept; Students Determine the Attributes

Lesson Step	Explanatory Notes for the Teacher
1. Identify the essential attributes that define or describe the concept you want to teach. Then create or locate examples and nonexamples that explicitly illustrate those characteristics. You can present examples in words, numbers, or pictures.	Choose examples that communicate the essence of the concept, and identify nonexamples that will stand out as polar opposites.
2. Model the concept attainment process for students using a familiar concept. Use the example in Column 2, or choose another that seems more pertinent to your students and content. Present the model concept to students, and show them examples and nonexamples.	Explain to students that all humans are constantly comparing what they experience to what they already know and deciding whether some new experience fits into Category A or B. Think, for example, of all the different representations of dogs that young children encounter: cartoons, actual dogs on the street, pictures of various breeds of dogs, and jewelry in the shape of a dog. How do they know to call all of these versions "a dog"? They know what the critical attributes of a dog are. In other words, they have "attained the concept" of a dog. You want your students to attain a concept so that when they encounter various representations of that concept, they will immediately recognize it is an example or a nonexample.
3. Explain the purpose of this technique to your students. Let them know that this technique is another way of comparing and contrasting two things so they can "attain a concept."	For this technique to be effective, students must be able to understand what is happening and why. Before you actually engage in a concept attainment lesson, model the process for students using familiar information.
4. After you model the process using a concept of your own choosing and explain the purpose of the technique, introduce the concept you are using for your concept attainment lesson.	Do not be tempted to speed up the process by skipping over modeling and demonstrating how the process works, or explaining to students what a concept attainment lesson is all about; help them to understand and remember what they learn.
5. Present your students with a clear example of the concept and a definitive nonexample of the concept.	Your examples can be pictures, definitions, equations, objects, or any other artifacts that are applicable to the concept, your information, and your students.

(continued on next page)

Table 3.2: Teacher Names the Concept; Students Determine the Attributes *(continued)*

6. Ask students to generate and test hypotheses about the attributes of the concept, based on the example or nonexample presented.	Generating a hypothesis requires that students make informed guesses about the attributes of the concept, based on what they observe about the example and what they cannot observe about the nonexample.
7. Present another example or nonexample to the class, and once again ask students to figure out the critical attribute(s) of the concept.	Either confirm your students' hypotheses, or ask them to provide more examples without naming a specific attribute so that other students may continue to work on the answer.
8. Either confirm students' hypotheses or have them provide examples without naming the attribute so that others may continue to work at it.	Continue presenting examples until all of the relevant attributes have been enumerated. Encourage discussion provoked by differences of opinion between class members.
9. Ask students to record their definitions in their academic or content vocabulary notebooks.	Be sure to provide enough time needed for students to record and represent the cognitive processing that has taken place during this technique. Encourage them to list all the attributes that they identified and to continue thinking about the concept to see if they might discover additional attributes to use the next time they make an entry in their notebooks.

Once students experience the first version of concept attainment as described in the previous lesson, consider graduating to the more cognitively complex version. In this version, the one that is most nearly like the work of Jerome Bruner (1973), students engage in what is called *inductive reasoning*, drawing conclusions and making generalizations from very specific observations that they make about the attributes of the concepts you present in examples and nonexamples. Table 3.3 contains a lesson plan for teaching this second version.

**Table 3.3: Teacher Provides Examples/Nonexamples
and Students Identify the Concept**

Lesson Step	Explanatory Information for the Teacher
1. Identify the critical attributes that define the concept or term, and then come up with clear examples that illustrate each attribute and a corresponding nonexample of the attribute.	The key to the success of your concept attainment lesson is the selection of definitive examples and nonexamples.
2. If your students are lower elementary, model this concept attainment using a familiar concept.	Keep it simple, particularly for younger children. Practice with familiar ideas so students understand the process before moving to concepts from critical content.
3. Introduce the purpose of this concept attainment lesson: students must use their reasoning powers to make inferences about a "mystery concept."	If you have previously used the simpler version of the process with your students, point out that they will need to become word detectives to figure out the mystery word or concept from the clues you present in the form of examples and nonexamples of the concept.
4. Present the first example or nonexample, and explain to the class that one is an example of the "mystery term or concept," and the other is not an example of the concept.	Of course, you will not reveal the concept at this time, and you may treat the lesson like a game if you prefer. Remind your students of the meaning of the term *nonexample* so you can readily use it without confusion on their part.
5. Direct students to generate and test their hypotheses about the attributes or the concepts.	Use this sentence stem to test their examples: Only some examples of the concept have the nondefining attribute, but all examples of the concept have the defining attribute. Substitute your concept and its attributes in the sentence stem to test your hypothesis. For example: Only some examples of impressionistic art have ballet dancers as subjects, but all examples of impressionistic art have subtle and blurry lines, giving off a foggy effect.

(continued on next page)

Table 3.3: Teacher Provides Examples/Nonexamples and Students Identify the Concept *(continued)*

6. Present another example or nonexample, and direct students to make an informed guess about the mystery concept.	If students are having a difficult time with this process, go back to your familiar concept and re-explain the difference between example and nonexample. These terms are sometimes confusing to students. Each of the examples must highlight a discrete, unambiguous characteristic of the concept you are teaching. Examples that are too general or unfamiliar can mislead or blur students' understanding.
7. Either confirm students' hypotheses or ask them to provide examples without naming the concept.	Do not give up the exercise too soon. Some students will need more time to work at it.
8. Continue presenting examples until the concept is identified. Encourage discussion over disagreements, and give all students opportunities to question and puzzle through the correct answer.	Encourage students to work together to provide clues and motivation.
9. Direct students to record their own definition of the concept as well as the attributes enumerated in the activity.	You may wish to keep a running list of the attributes on a piece of chart paper or the board so students can refer to it as they make notes in their academic or content vocabulary notebooks.

Common Mistakes

Following are some all-too-common mistakes that can creep into a concept attainment lesson:

- The teacher permits students to use nondefining attributes to describe the concept, instead of using only defining attributes.

- The teacher does not select strong examples for a concept attainment activity.

- The teacher makes the concept too complicated.

- The teacher does not place the examples in a precise sequence in order to reveal and reinforce attributes one at a time.

Examples and Nonexamples of Processing New Information Using Concept Attainment

The following examples and nonexamples demonstrate how to process new information using concept attainment.

Elementary Example of Processing New Information Concept Attainment

The learning target for this example is *distinguish between defining attributes versus non-defining attributes* (CCSS.Math-Content.1.G.A.1).

The first-grade teacher knows that his students can recognize and name basic shapes, but he wants to deepen their understanding by giving them additional practice in identifying attributes to have them come up with their own definition for two shapes: triangle and rectangle. He decides to use a concept attainment approach.

> Boys and girls, today I'm going to ask you to be mathematicians and come up with an exact definition of a rectangle. You will work together to look at some pictures that I will show you. The pictures will help you answer the question, what is a rectangle?

The teacher shows the class a set of two rectangles different in size from each other and says, "These are both rectangles." Then the teacher shows two nonexamples, one a three-sided figure and the second a five-sided figure, and says, "These are not rectangles."

He pauses to allow students time for processing. "Now talk to your partner about what you notice about the rectangles that you do not see in the nonexample." The teacher goes on to present two more rectangles different in orientation: one sideways, one tilted. The two nonexamples he presents are a trapezoid and a rhombus. He says, "Compare the figures in the example and the figures in the nonexample. What do you notice?"

The teacher presents one more set of examples and nonexamples. By this time, most students are able to conclude that a rectangle has four sides and square corners. However, some students are certain that a rectangle has to be "lying on its side." The teacher redirects their attention to the first pair of rectangles he showed them. He prompts students using a sentence stem: "Only some of the rectangles are lying on their sides, but all of the rectangles have four sides and four square corners."

Students are able to see their flawed thinking. By the end of class, the students are able to summarize the *defining* characteristics (defining attributes) of a rectangle as a four-sided figure with four square corners.

Elementary Nonexample of Concept Attainment

The learning target for this example is *distinguish between defining attributes versus non-defining attributes* (CCSS.Math-Content.1.G.A.1).

The nonexample teacher is planning a hands-on concept attainment activity with the triangle shape. He gives each group a bucket of pattern blocks, a box of attribute blocks, and a set of Tangrams and introduces his lesson:

> You are going to be "Math Explorers" today and explore shapes. Out of all these shapes, I want you to pick out the triangles and put them together. Then I want each group to tell me three things you know about triangles.

Students work quickly, sorting out all triangles from the three sets of manipulatives. When the teacher checks in with one group, the students are insistent that triangles have three sides, are usually green, and come in three sizes: small, medium, and large. The teacher quickly realizes to his dismay that the materials provided too many options and many were confusing to students. The group's definition of a triangle would not hold up for all possible triangles. The teacher realizes that he failed to achieve the desired result with his lesson.

Secondary Example of Concept Attainment

The learning target of this secondary example is *analyze and interpret data on natural hazards to forecast future catastrophic events and inform the development of technologies to mitigate their effects* (Next Generation Science Standards, MS-ESS3-2 Earth and Human Activity). A middle school science teacher creates a unit of study on the topic of natural hazards. She introduces the activity:

> We have been learning about major natural hazards and disasters that have happened globally over the last ten years. I want to help you deepen your understanding of the concept of "natural hazards" by playing a game called Ins and Outs. The objective of the game is for you to determine the attributes of a natural hazard. First, I'm going to give you an example of a natural hazard—that's an "In" because it fits in the category. Then, I'm going to give you a nonexample—an "Out." It does not fit into the category of natural hazards. Now, don't assume that because it doesn't fit, we can't learn from it. After each pair, you are going to work with your partner to list any attributes you think must be present for an example to be called a *natural hazard*. When you think you have figured out the attribute, don't call it out but instead, give us an example of an "In" and an "Out." I'll tell you if you're correct, and you can continue to give examples and nonexamples for the rest of the class to keep guessing.

The teacher wants all students to determine features based on the following attributes she has identified in advance: 1) amount of immediate destruction, 2) predictability, and 3) causes and correlations. The paired list she developed in advance includes the examples and nonexamples shown in Figure 3.1.

Figure 3.1: Ins and Outs From the Secondary Example Lesson

INs This Is IN (example)	OUTs This Is OUT (nonexample)
Volcano	Geyser
Flood	Ocean tides
Tornado	Explosion
Earthquake	Eclipse
Landslide	Bridge collapse

The teacher has some evocative questions ready to ask students when they think they have determined accurate attributes. She asks, "What about a drought? Would you call that an 'In' or an 'Out'? What about a forest fire? An oil spill?" The students went on to create a list of attributes from this activity. Figure 3.2 displays their list.

Figure 3.2: List of Defining Attributes for a Natural Hazard

1. *much destruction results*
2. *happens in the natural world*
3. *caused by weather, geology, or humans*
4. *can be either somewhat predictable or totally unpredictable*

At the end of the lesson, the teacher asks students to write their own definitions of a *natural hazard* and list its defining attributes. Teacher and students agree that the best part of the lesson is the friendly controversy that occurs during the discussion about whether an oil spill is a natural hazard. Some students want to change their definitions at that point, and others argue that it fits the criteria they have determined.

Secondary Nonexample of Processing New Information Using Concept Attainment

The learning target of this secondary example is *analyze and interpret data on natural hazards to forecast future catastrophic events and inform the development of technologies to mitigate their effects* (Next Generation Science Standards, MS-ESS3-2 Earth and Human Activity). The teacher decides to use a concept attainment lesson similar to the one the example teacher uses. But this teacher rushes in his preparation for the lesson and does not spend the time needed to develop a clear-cut set of example and nonexample photos to show his students. And to further complicate his lesson, he does not have a well-conceived list of attributes developed in advance. His students pick up on the teacher's confusion, and when they disagree with him about the various natural hazards, he cuts the lesson short.

Determining If Students Can Process New Information Using Concept Attainment

Monitoring the extent to which students can actively process new information during concept attainment activities is critical to the effectiveness of this technique. Here are some behaviors to monitor:

- Students are able to verbalize their understanding of new information by describing or defining a given concept.

- Students are able to create lists of attributes to describe a given concept.

- Students can generate sets of examples and nonexamples to illustrate a given concept.

- Students are able to compare examples and nonexamples showing an understanding of the defining and nondefining attributes.

- Students can record their deeper understanding of a concept after engaging in concept attainment.

- Students can explain what is and what is not an example of a concept and explain why.

Table 3.4 displays a student proficiency scale for processing new information using concept attainment. Use it to determine the progression of your students' abilities to achieve the desired result.

Table 3.4: Student Proficiency Scale for Processing New Information Using Concept Attainment

Emerging	Fundamental	Desired Result
Students identify attributes of examples.	Students identify defining attributes of examples.	Students relate the defining attributes of the examples to the concept.
Students identify common attributes among the examples.	Students identify the concept, given examples and nonexamples of the attributes.	Students identify the concept and explain how the common attributes helped them identify it.
	Students brainstorm other possible examples of the concept.	Students generate other accurate examples of the concept.

Scaffold and Extend Instruction to Meet Students' Needs

Here are some ways to scaffold and extend instruction for students who need extra support or enhanced instruction during the implementation of concept attainment:

Scaffolding

- Model the process using familiar concepts with very obvious examples and nonexamples.

- Use the first version of the concept attainment technique to scaffold students' understanding of the exercise.

- Provide more hints and obvious clues while students are learning the process.

- Partner with two struggling students while the remainder of the class works on some aspect of the concept attainment technique.

Extending

- Make attributes more cognitively demanding.

- Provide fewer attributes with less scaffolding.

- Encourage students to use secondary resources to support generalizations.

- Allow students to add additional attributes to both the examples and nonexamples.

- Encourage students to create their own examples and nonexamples that can be shared with the class at a later time.

Instructional Technique 4

USING JIGSAW

Instructional Technique 4 is an active processing technique called Jigsaw. Elliot Aronson and his university students developed this method in the 1970s as a way to reduce conflict or competition and increase cooperation in classrooms, particularly in areas of the country where bringing diverse student groups together constituted new school communities (Aronson & Patnoe, 2011). After thirty years of research in various settings and daily use in schools, it retains its popularity among teachers looking for an organized way to facilitate collaborative processing of new information. A critical attribute of the Jigsaw process that distinguishes it from other methods is the degree of interdependence among students that it requires and ultimately fosters in your classroom over time. As the term *jigsaw* suggests, each member of the collaborative group holds a single piece of a puzzle in the form of new information. The group can only process the information in its entirety when the group members come together to share the results of their individual processing of a single chunk of information. Only as the result of collaboration and interdependence can the group assemble the big picture.

How to Effectively Implement Processing New Information Using Jigsaw

The effective implementation of this technique requires learning the steps of the Jigsaw process so you can teach and model it for your students. Many educators and researchers have developed variations of the process, but there are two basic versions.

The process works best with new information or text material that you divide into a number of chunks equal to the number of students in each jigsaw group. The word *jigsaw* suggests how this technique works with your students. Each member of a jigsaw group becomes an expert on one assigned chunk of new information. As the teacher progresses through the lesson, stopping after each chunk of information input, each student in the group of three has an opportunity to act as the expert by sharing some aspect of the new information. At the end of the lesson, the pieces or chunks of information fit together to complete the Jigsaw as well as summarize the new information for a particular period.

Each member needs the other to process new information. For instance, after previewing a brief introductory video on the scientific method, students divide into groups of three. Then, you assign students one of the first three steps of the scientific method. The first student becomes the expert on the first step. The second student becomes the expert on the second step, and the third student becomes the expert on the third step. The group members are allowed to *individually* process their chunk and then share what they have learned with each other. Table 4.1 enumerates the steps in this streamlined version. In this version, the "experts" work on their own before rejoining the other members of their group. This version is ideal to use with a more homogeneous group of advanced students whom you expect to bring similar levels of processing to their chunk of the text, resulting in a whole-group product that represents the information more accurately.

Table 4.1: The Streamlined Version of Jigsaw

Lesson Step	Explanatory Notes for the Teacher
1. Select the information or text materials you wish to use for the Jigsaw process. Decide what type of template or task you will assign each student or group.	This process is more suited to the active processing of text than a teacher presentation.
2. Divide the information or text into as many chunks as you have students in each group.	Try to make the chunks about equal in size so that the process does not bog down.
3. Assign each student a chunk to individually process.	This streamlined version requires that students work independently on processing their chunk. Use more familiar topics or easier text when you introduce this process for the first time.
4. Give students time to read and process their assigned chunks.	Students with reading difficulties may need easier reading content text.
5. Regroup and direct students to share their ideas with their groups.	Monitor the sharing to ensure productive collaboration.
6. Ask the groups to summarize the big picture of the information they processed.	Collect the summary product you assigned to determine whether they achieved the desired result.

The second version of the Jigsaw process solves the problem in the first version, as noted earlier: students are expected to read and process the information or text independently. Using the earlier example of students processing the three steps of the scientific method, all of the students you assigned as "experts" to actively process step one of the scientific method gather in an "expert group" for about ten minutes. This meeting provides an opportunity for students to clarify and fine-tune their "expertise" before rejoining their original groups and sharing their knowledge. Back in their "home group," each student will have a turn at sharing the insights and information they have absorbed from the "expert group." Table 4.2 enumerates the steps in the expert group version of the Jigsaw process.

Table 4.2: The Expert Group Version of Jigsaw

Lesson Step	Explanatory Notes for the Teacher
1. Directly teach the Jigsaw method to students.	Teach students what it means to be an expert. Provide explicit instructions on 1) becoming an expert, 2) using resources to assist in acquiring critical information, 3) sharing your expert knowledge with your collaborative team, and 4) the method they will need to record and represent knowledge the experts provide.
2. Assign appropriate chunks of information, and allow adequate time for processing.	Work with expert groups to ensure they are adequately discussing and sharing what they know with other experts. Be ready to facilitate any disagreements about the accuracy of information, and be sure to make corrections if needed before the students share misinformation with other group members.
3. Choose primary resources to facilitate processing.	Provide adequate primary and secondary resources for students to search for additional background on their new information.
4. Monitor for active processing.	Make a checklist of ways you plan to monitor your students to determine the extent to which they achieve the desired result.
5. Assess learning of new information.	Provide a formal or informal means to assess learning.

When you implement this process correctly, it allows each student to present and receive information and fosters student autonomy—a critical component required for rigorous instruction. The adequate amount of time needed to achieve the desired result varies depending on the cognitive demand of the information chunks.

Common Mistakes

Having advance warning of potential mistakes that may occur during the implementation of a technique saves time and resources. The consideration of common mistakes in advance also allows teachers to determine necessary adaptations needed for learners. There are four potential problems that can arise as the teacher uses the Jigsaw process:

- The teacher fails to teach and model the appropriate steps of the process.

- The teacher fails to teach and model the necessary expert and group responsibilities.

- The teacher fails to select appropriate amounts of information for each group member to process.

- The teacher does not provide adequate support during the times when students are collaboratively processing assigned chunks of new information.

Examples and Nonexamples of Collaboratively Processing New Information Using Jigsaw in the Classroom

The following classroom examples and nonexamples offer you an opportunity to sit in on some teachers who are using the Jigsaw technique. As you read the scenarios, listen to the teachers' voices and consider a model to emulate, and take note of which practices you will seek to avoid.

Elementary Example of Processing New Information Using Jigsaw

The learning target for this example is *explain how a series of chapters, scenes, or stanzas fits together to provide the overall structure of a particular story, drama, or poem* (CCSS.ELA-Literacy.RL5.5).

Written on the board are the steps of the Jigsaw process:

1. Entire class: Read the poem.

2. In your first group: Study your assigned stanza and answer the questions.

3. In your second group: Discuss the answer to the questions for each stanza in order.

4. Individually: Summarize how stanzas fit together to provide the overall structure of this poem and how the structure relates to the experience the author wants to convey.

Good morning, class. Today our learning target is to explain how the stanzas of a poem fit together to provide the overall structure of a poem. This poem will help us answer our essential question, "How does the structure of a text impact a reader's experience and understanding of a text?"

"The Echoing Green" is a classic poem by William Blake. We will use this poem to determine how the stanzas provide information about the structure of poetry and how it relates to the experience the author wants to convey to the reader.

To do this, we will follow the steps for a Jigsaw that are on the board. First, we will read the poem silently. Then, I will read the poem aloud. So let's do that before we continue.

The teacher walks around as students silently read, helping them with words they do not understand and checking that all students are reading. She then reads the poem aloud, stopping periodically to ask questions and clarify some of the language.

Now I will assign one stanza to each collaborative group of three, and this will be your first group. Study your stanza. To become an "expert" on your stanza, answer the questions on the processing template and discuss the stanza with your group.

1. Is there a pattern to the number of lines in your stanza?

2. Is there repetition of words, phrases, sounds, or rhythms?

3. Are there any unique grammatical strategies in your stanza?

4. Are there any specific visuals that you imagine as you read your stanza?

As the students complete this, the teacher walks around reading the answers students are writing and asking clarifying questions. As well, she listens to discussions to ensure accuracy from the "experts."

> Now that you have completed that step, we will rearrange the groups so that you will each take your expertise to your second (expert) group, where you will engage in a detailed discussion about how the stanza all the members of your group studied relates to the overall structure of the poem. Use your answers to the questions to guide your conversation. Use the processing template to assist you with recording your observations and your partners' observations.

The teacher once again walks around reading answers, asking clarifying questions, and listening to discussions to ensure accuracy from the experts.

> As our last step in the Jigsaw, summarize how the stanzas fit together to provide the overall structure of this poem and how the structure relates to the experience the author wants to convey.

The teacher reads over students' shoulders as they write their summaries and then collects these summaries to check for accuracy.

Elementary Nonexample of Processing
New Information Using Jigsaw

The learning target for this example is *explain how a series of chapters, scenes, or stanzas fits together to provide the overall structure of a particular story, drama, or poem* (CCSS.ELA-Literacy.RL5.5). The teacher begins the lesson:

> Good morning, class. Today we will "Jigsaw" a poem by William Blake called "The Echoing Green." Each person will individually read the poem and then discuss with their home group how each stanza relates to the structure of the poem. Remember, a poem's structure clues the reader in to the author's purpose for writing the poem. You all have five minutes to read the poem on your own, write a summary of each stanza, and then write a summary of how the author uses the poem's structure to convey meaning. After your five minutes are up, I will ask you to share your summary with your group. You don't have to write down what your partners say, because they might be wrong. Just make sure you listen as they talk. I will walk around and monitor how well you quietly listen to your partners' summaries.

Our nonexample does not provide support for learners who need to hear the teacher read the poem aloud. There is also no responsibility to the group. The activity allows students quiet time to read and summarize information with little to no accountability to their team. Various perspectives are not considered, and students have no opportunity to work with their peers to actively ask and answer questions about the new information.

Secondary Example of Processing New Information Using Jigsaw

The learning target for this secondary example is *solve systems of linear equations in two variables algebraically and graphically* (CCSS.Math-Algebra. REI.6).

The middle school algebra teacher is exploring how to help his students more deeply understand the various ways to solve systems of linear equations. He has taught each of the methods but notices that his students frequently fall back on the same method. He decides to use the Jigsaw process to give his students the opportunity to become an "expert" in one of the methods to teach it to other students. He decides to focus on the three algebraic methods for the process: inspection, elimination, and substitution. He experiments with various groups and assigns the easiest method, *inspection*, to the individual in each group who is having the most difficulty, theorizing that this student could really benefit from some expert instruction in the other two methods but needs to have at least one method down solidly. Having made that decision, putting the rest of the groups together falls into place. Here is how he introduces the Jigsaw method to his class.

Good afternoon, class. We're going to change things up a bit today. I'm taking the day off from teaching algebra, and I've recruited a group of highly knowledgeable experts. That would be you. We're going to use the Jigsaw process that we used several times at the beginning of the semester. But, in case you've forgotten, I've posted the steps in the process. And, I've also posted a list of the home groups. With each name, I've written the method the individual will use to solve these equations:

$$2p + 2k = 360$$

$$3p + 2k = 414$$

The teacher points to the steps:

1. Meet with your home group, and find out which method you have been assigned to solve the system of linear equations.

2. See if you can solve the equation on your own.

3. If you cannot, consult some of the resources I've put together for you: a link to a YouTube video demonstrating your method, a copy of the study guide I prepared for you earlier, and a printout describing the three methods in more detail.

4. Solve the problem using your resources.

> Leave your home group and join your "expert" group. All the students in this group have been solving the same problem using the same method. Put your heads together. If you had trouble solving your problem, find an expert in the group to help you so you will be able to explain your method to your home group.
>
> When all expert groups have shared their expertise, all students return to their home group. Each of the three students takes a turn teaching the assigned method.
>
> Each home group summarizes its experiences on a summary sheet, showing the three different solutions the group obtained.
>
> Are there any questions about the process? Now, this could get complicated, so listen carefully. There are eighteen students, and that gives us six home groups. With six home groups we will have six experts in each group—a group of six experts at using the method.

While groups are working, the teacher deliberately monitors the "expert" groups to ensure they understand their steps. This monitoring doubles as an informal means to assess students' learning. Once the experts return to their home groups, he again carefully monitors the groups to listen in on their presentations of how they solved the system of linear equations.

At the close of the lesson, the teacher collects the summary sheet from each home group. The lesson took a great deal of advance thought and planning, but as he looks over the summary sheets and thinks about how his struggling students really came alive in this process, he feels it was worth every minute of planning and class time.

Secondary Nonexample of Processing
New Information Using Jigsaw

The learning target for this secondary nonexample is *solve systems of linear equations in two variables algebraically and graphically* (CCSS.Math-Algebra.REI.6).

The nonexample teacher has observed her colleague across the hall using the Jigsaw process to develop deeper understandings of relatively new content information. She is intrigued and consults with him to learn about the details of the process. Once she begins planning her lesson, her fears emerge about the time this will take away from covering the content and all of the work involved in putting together a set of resources for each method, so she decides to take some shortcuts. Her colleague recommends that before using it for new content, she give her students some basic training in how the process works and the reasons for using it, but she knows her students have engaged in collaborative processing in other classes and feels they will readily adapt in her classroom.

As she delivers the lesson, the unavailability of expert resources for students who need to work individually before joining the expert group frustrates many students. Finally, students are not quite clear about the sudden change in the class structure. They are accustomed to taking notes as the teacher lectures and have difficulty sharing their perspectives with others.

Determining If Students Can Process New Information Using Jigsaw

As the final step in the implementation of the Jigsaw process, take time to monitor that your students accomplish two things: 1) they understand the power of collaboration for solving problems and processing new information and 2) they have sufficiently processed new content information. Here are some behaviors that effective teachers can monitor:

- Students can provide an exit ticket explaining the main ideas presented by each group member or a summary of all learned information.

- Students can engage in a whole-group discussion in which the teacher carefully notes the depth of their information.

- Students chosen randomly from each group share information presented from an expert in their group.

- Students can make corrections or ask the teacher for clarification.

- Students assume ownership of their responsibility as group members in both their home groups and their expert groups.

- Students ask each other pertinent questions about the information during both their home groups and their expert groups.

- Students can verbally explain what they learned.

- Students can actively discuss and report the information from other experts.

- Students ask each other questions about the information and generate conclusions.

- Students readily teach their assigned content and eagerly learn content from other home team members.

Table 4.3 displays a student proficiency scale for processing new information using the Jigsaw process. Use it to plan for instruction that targets the desired result.

Table 4.3: Student Proficiency Scale for Processing New Information Using the Jigsaw Method

Emerging	Fundamental	Desired Result
Students participate in a discussion about the assigned chunk of content.	Students discuss their perspectives about the assigned chunk of content.	Students discuss multiple perspectives to summarize the assigned chunk of content.
Students explain information from the assigned chunk of content.	Students identify and explain critical information from the assigned chunk of content.	Students accurately explain details of the critical information of the assigned chunk of content.
Students listen as others explain their assigned chunk of content.	Students discuss or ask questions about other students' explanations of their assigned chunk of content.	Students actively participate in a discussion about each chunk of content.
Students state conclusions about the content as a result of using Jigsaw.	Students generate their own conclusions about the content as a result of using Jigsaw.	Students include multiple perspectives in their own conclusions about the content as a result of using Jigsaw.

Scaffold and Extend Instruction to Meet Students' Needs

Scaffolding and extending instruction for your students can provide mutually beneficial experiences for struggling students who need additional opportunities to acquire the nuances of the Jigsaw process and also benefit students who have knowledge to share with their classmates.

Scaffolding

Here are some ways you can scaffold the Jigsaw technique for your students:

- Form a supportive Jigsaw group in which you provide more direct instruction about the process.

- Model and think aloud for students about how you would teach a chunk to the group.

- Provide opportunities to summarize and teach new information in visual ways as well as in oral or written formats.

- Provide think sheets or templates to guide students through the process.

- Provide easy reading or visual resources that can offer content expertise.

Extending

Here are two ways to extend instruction for students who need to be challenged by the critical content:

- Give students opportunities to determine how they wish to share and record their expertise.

- Encourage students who have advanced content knowledge to develop mini-videos or podcasts that summarize and draw conclusions about various chunks of content.

Instructional Technique 5

USING RECIPROCAL TEACHING

Reciprocal Teaching (RT), developed by Palinscar and Brown (1984), is a reading comprehension strategy that has been described or adapted in every major educational psychology and reading methods textbook. They developed RT as a way to support struggling readers in the comprehension of text. The strategy consists of the teacher directly instructing students in four cognitive/comprehension strategies—summarizing, questioning, predicting, and clarifying—while simultaneously training students to assume responsibilities for leading small-group discussions in the role of teacher. Implementation of this technique requires several instructional steps to include directly teaching and modeling for students how to employ the strategies in the reading of text and then teaching and coaching students in how to assume the role of teacher or discussion leader in a small group. Although they designed RT specifically for use in a small group of struggling students reading text together, this technique provides an adaptation for processing new information during oral teacher presentations as well as suggesting other possible adaptations.

How to Effectively Implement Processing New Information Using Reciprocal Teaching

The effective implementation of this technique requires a substantial commitment of instructional time and energy, especially if you have not had any preservice instruction or professional staff development regarding how to teach and model cognitive reading strategies. If you are currently implementing cognitive strategy instruction in your classroom, adapting RT will prove to be less time consuming. However, if you take the time to understand, teach, and model these cognitive processes for students, your investment will pay rich dividends in terms of student learning and achievement.

There are three steps to the effective implementation of RT: 1) be mindful and reflective of how you use the four cognitive processes in your own reading and thinking, 2) teach and model the four cognitive processes for your students, and 3) implement one or more of the various versions of the RT method.

Master the Four Cognitive Processes of RT

The first step to the effective implementation of RT is mastering the four cognitive processes and experimenting with them as they apply to your own thinking and reading. If you teach reading comprehension in your classroom, you will likely have enough background knowledge to make this first step nothing more than a quick review. However, bear in mind that if you have used different definitions or approaches for these processes in your classroom, you should continue to use terminology that your students have already mastered. Table 5.1 presents a set of definitions to scaffold your learning and teaching of the processes.

Teach and Model the Reciprocal Teaching Process for Your Students

Do not attempt to implement RT by simply telling your students to predict, question, clarify, and summarize. You might assume that since your students are in the upper elementary or secondary grades, they are quite familiar with the terms, can define them, can describe them, and actually know how to apply them in their reading and thinking. If so, you are most fortunate. However, if you want your students to routinely use these processes to assume a role as a leader or teacher of a small collaborative processing group, take the time to teach and model each cognitive process.

Modeling what a strategy sounds like can seem awkward and scripted, but until students can actually hear the words the teacher speaks, they will be less likely to assume the role comfortably. Figure 5.1 provides some examples of what each of the RT strategies might sound like in the context of a discussion. Use these suggestions to prepare your own think-alouds or share them as prompts to students who will be assuming the various roles or leading the discussion on their own.

Table 5.1: Definitions of the Four Cognitive Processes Used in Reciprocal Teaching

Definition of the Cognitive Process	Explanatory Notes for the Teacher
Predicting requires that listeners and readers make predictions about future information that involves them in drawing conclusions and testing their inferences. Predicting is essential for comprehension as learners continually test their hypotheses regarding what they think will happen against what is actually happening and then figuring out what to do if their predictions do not materialize.	Teachers often overlook prediction as an inferential process because they routinely facilitate predicting before reading text or predicting what will happen next in a narrative. However, a major aspect of predicting involves drawing conclusions and testing hypotheses that readers have made. As you model predicting for students, be sure to show the range of thinking that is involved in this strategy.
Summarizing in the context of RT can be viewed as a self-review activity in which readers/listeners continuously work on what the main idea of the information might be while not having trivial and unimportant information distract them.	Summarizing can involve either giving an oral summary of what has occurred or preparing a brief written summary about what is most important about a chunk of new information. As you present critical content to students, be sure that you intentionally identify the critical information. Put yourself in the place of your students who are trying to answer questions about what's important. If you often get lost in trivia and sidetracked by extraneous information, your students will be unable to successfully summarize new information you have presented.
Clarifying in the context of RT is a self-monitoring process: being aware that reading or thinking has gone off track and some action needs to be taken to get back on track. Clarifying is fixing up the mix-ups that often occur when reading challenging text. Asking students to clarify requires that they engage in critical evaluation as they read, not only for the content itself but also a self-evaluation of their personal comprehension.	If your students are having difficulty with monitoring, prepare a set of clarifying tools. For example, suggest that students do the following when they are confused about the meaning of the text: 1) read the text again or even twice more; 2) stop and think aloud to themselves about what they have read; 3) talk to someone: think aloud to a friend, family member, classmate, or the teacher; or 4) ignore temporarily the parts they do not understand, and keep reading.
Questioning in the context of RT involves students generating questions after they first identify significant content. Posing questions is a way to self-test one's understanding of the content since often the individual posing the question already has a good idea of what the answer might be. Questions direct the questioner to identify the main idea.	Questions can be factual or inferential and draw the questioner into forecasting the types of questions the teacher might ask on a test of the new information.

Definitions adapted from Palinscar & Brown (1984). Explanatory notes for the teacher are original to the authors.

Figure 5.1: Examples of What the RT Strategies Sound Like

Strategy	What Does This Strategy Sound Like?
Predicting	"I think that this article will tell us about . . . because I looked at the headings and subheadings in the text." "I was surprised by what happened, and I later changed my mind because . . ." "I believe that this story is not imagined, but real." "I think this author is an expert on the subject, and we will have to pay close attention to understand the information." "I think this must be what the author means. Let's keep on reading and see if I'm right."
Summarizing	"The big idea of this chunk is . . ." "I think that this story is mainly about . . ." "The most important thing about . . . is . . ." "Let's go back and look at the topic sentence." "We're paying too much attention to unimportant information." "We have to keep answering the question, what is the central idea?"
Clarifying	"Wait a minute. I'm confused. Can we figure out the meaning of this word before we go on?" "I think there's a clue in the context here that will help us figure out what that means." "Can we go back and reread that sentence again?" "Can we draw a picture or diagram of that?"
Questioning	"How does this information fit with what we learned last week? I don't see the connection." "Where can we find more information about this subject?" "What does the text mean when it says . . . ?" "Does anyone remember what we learned about this topic last year?" "Can anyone tell me why we are learning about this?"

Implement Reciprocal Teaching or One of Its Adaptations

Educators believe that lesson plans are meant to be adapted, and if imitation is the sincerest form of flattery, RT has been flattered by the best. Table 5.2 describes the original and some of its adaptations.

Table 5.2: Reciprocal Teaching and Its Adaptations

Version	Description
Palinscar & Brown (1984)	Palinscar and Brown developed this original version of RT for struggling readers. They hypothesized that if students were intentionally taught four reading/cognitive strategies and then trained to use them in a collaborative, student-led group, their reading comprehension would improve. This was indeed the case, and the study launched an intensive interest in directly teaching reading comprehension strategies to students.
Strong et al. (2002)	Strong and his colleagues tweaked the Palinscar & Brown model by dropping the clarifying strategy and substituting managing new vocabulary as the fourth strategy.
Fisher, Frey & Lapp (2012)	Fisher, Frey, and Lapp further adapted the RT model by eliminating the student discussion leader and assigning roles to students corresponding to the four cognitive strategies: predictor, question generator, summarizer, and clarifier. Students are taught all of the roles and take turns assuming them during the reading of different chunks of the text.
Marzano & Boogren (2012)	Marzano and Boogren adapted the RT method for processing chunks of teacher-presented content. They retained the student teacher/discussion leader to facilitate the process. Table 5.3 presents the steps in this adaptation for processing teacher-presented content. Table 5.4 presents the Marzano and Boogren adaptation for reading chunks of content text.

Table 5.3 presents a step-by-step collaborative processing lesson using RT to process new content information the teacher presents. The role of the student leader and the expectations for the group members are explicitly delineated. You could use this table as a template for training students for the various roles they will play during the process, while Table 5.2, shown earlier, could be used for showing students examples of the various RT strategies.

Table 5.3: Using RT to Process New Information from Teacher-Presented Content

Lesson Step
1. The teacher presents a chunk of new information.
2. The student teacher (discussion leader) generates questions to ask his group about the information. The members of his group discuss answers to the question(s).
3. The student teacher asks a member of his group to summarize the information presented thus far.
4. As needed, the student teacher asks the members of his group if there are any terms or concepts that need clarifying before they move on. Then, the student teacher might restate or paraphrase the new information.
5. The members of the group make predictions about the information of the upcoming chunk.
6. The teacher presents another chunk of information, and each of the groups in the classroom once again go through the processes of questioning, summarizing, clarifying, and predicting.
7. The teacher directs each group to list some conclusions they have made about the new information or a summary statement of the most important information in the teacher's presentation.

Adapted from Marzano & Boogren (2012).

Table 5.4 adapts the RT method in Table 5.3 to collaboratively process the reading of content text.

Table 5.4: Using RT to Process New Information from the Reading of Content Text

Lesson Step
1. The teacher assigns text for students to read. The reading method can vary as dictated by the needs of the students and the difficulty of the text. However, the teacher must chunk the text in advance so that students do not experience cognitive overload.
2. The student teacher (discussion leader) generates questions to ask his group about the information. The members of his group discuss answers to the question(s).
3. The student teacher asks a member of the group to summarize the information presented this far.
4. As needed, the student teacher asks the members of his group if there are any terms or concepts that need clarifying before they move on. Then, the student teacher might restate or paraphrase the new information.
5. The members of the group make predictions about the information of the upcoming chunk.
6. The students read another chunk of information, and each of the groups in the classroom once again go through the processes of questioning, summarizing, clarifying, and predicting. This process continues through all the chunks of text.
7. The group develops a summary statement that represents the big idea of the text.

Adapted from Marzano & Boogren (2012).

Common Mistakes

Here are the most common mistakes the teacher might make when using the RT method to process new information with her students:

- The teacher fails to teach and model the RT strategies for students in advance of attempting the implementation.

- The teacher fails to teach and coach students as they assume the role of discussion leaders.

- The teacher fails to provide appropriately sized chunks of information of text or orally presented information.

- The teacher fails to provide appropriate levels of support for students who may have reading difficulties.

- The teacher fails to provide adequate time for processing and discussion during each phase of the method.

- The teacher fails to organize appropriate groups for processing.

Examples and Nonexamples of Processing New Knowledge Using Reciprocal Teaching

As you consider these examples and nonexamples, read carefully to recognize the common mistakes and make connections to the suggestions for how to effectively implement reciprocal teaching.

Elementary Example of Processing New Information Using the Reciprocal Teaching Method

The learning target of this elementary example is *the solar system consists of planets and other bodies that orbit the sun in predictable paths* (Science Community Representing Education [SCORE] Standards for Fifth Grade, Earth Sciences 5).

> Good morning, class. Today we will learn about our solar system. It consists of planets and other bodies that orbit the sun in predictable paths. I will be presenting three chunks of very important information about our solar system, and after each chunk, you are going to get into your RT groups to process the new information. Check the chart on the back wall to find out who will be the student teacher of each group and which table in the classroom will be your home base. Before we begin talking about the solar system, I'd like to review the four strategies that you will be using in your groups to process the new information.

The teacher walks over to the RT chart on the back wall and points out the descriptions of *questioning, predicting, summarizing,* and *clarifying.* She explains that she has prepared a handout with some sentence stems and prompts for the student teachers to use while they are leading the discussions in each group. She reminds students that their job during the information input is to listen for important information that will be discussed during the

RT session. The discussion leader is the only person permitted to take notes. She then begins her first ten-minute chunk of information input. After her presentation, she prompts students to get into their RT groups and walks around the room to make sure that each group of four students and the designated student teacher for the day are ready. She gives the groups one last chance to ask any questions they have about the discussion procedure and explains the timelines.

Since the information input was relatively short, her students have seen her model the strategies, and the student teachers have been trained and selected by the teacher for the first few RT sessions, she is feeling quite confident. Her extensive planning and preparation are paying off.

Elementary Nonexample of Reciprocal Teaching

The learning target of this elementary nonexample is *the solar system consists of planets and other bodies that orbit the sun in predictable paths* (SCORE Standards for Fifth Grade, Earth Sciences 5).

Our elementary nonexample teacher provides the primary resource for the students and directs students to use the RT method. However, critical levels of support are missing. The teacher does not group students for collaboration, no assistance is provided for their questions and clarifications, no expectation is set for monitoring their summaries, and he provides minimal time for students to read the text and generate conclusions. The teacher realizes the time restraint. However, instead of using a different processing technique, he tells the students to complete the *prediction* and *questioning* steps and skip the summary requirement this time. Students hurry through the process knowing that the teacher will not collect their work and review it for accuracy.

Secondary Example of Processing New Information Using Reciprocal Teaching

The learning target for this secondary example is *understand the "Second Reconstruction" and its advancement of civil rights; evaluate the Warren Court's reasoning in* Brown v. Board of Education *and its significance in advancing civil rights* (National History Standards for Grades 5–12, Standard 4A).

The high school history teacher in this example plans a lesson in which her students will use the RT method to read and process a primary source document: the original Supreme Court decision of *Brown v. Board of Education*. She plans to read aloud short segments of each chunk to get students started and then expects the small groups to chorally read the challenging text. She has previously taught and modeled the RT process for her students and earlier in the week practiced the process using a short article containing background information about the case. She has divided her class into groups of five and designated three student leaders for each group. A different student leader will be in charge for each chunk of text. She introduces her lesson:

> Good morning, class. Today we will learn about a landmark civil rights case that altered our nation's education system: *Brown v. Board of Education of Topeka, Kansas.* You will use the RT method as you read the text of this case. Let's take a minute to review the steps you will use in your groups of five. *[The steps the teacher has posted on the wall are similar to those in Table 5.4 found earlier in the technique.]*
>
> *[The teacher then explains the timeline she has developed for the process.]*
>
> When you are finished, post your summaries on the large chart paper and hang them around the room. We will conduct a gallery walk at the end of class.

Secondary Nonexample of Processing New Information Using Reciprocal Teaching

The secondary nonexample teacher believes that students should read independently, which can be appropriate; however, many students gain a deeper understanding when sharing and hearing other peer perspectives. Independent reading can be followed by time for collaboration. The teacher also assumes that the information is easily "digestible" and does not allow adequate processing time to complete each step. It will be difficult for students to achieve the desired result of summarizing and generating conclusions about the landmark case if they cannot read the information. Readers who need support may struggle. Students who have difficulty with reading fluency may benefit from being partnered with a fluent reader. Fluent readers may read critical pieces of the text aloud. The teacher may assist struggling readers by reading the text aloud to them.

> Good morning, class. Today we're going to learn about a landmark civil rights case that affected the education system in our nation: *Brown v. Board of Education of Topeka, Kansas.* We will use the RT method to engage in this lesson after you read the text independently. You have twenty minutes to complete the steps of the RT method. Use your chart to show your work for each step. After twenty minutes, we will have a group discussion about your summaries. Please do this in a timely fashion. I want us to complete the task in time. Let me know if you need my help. I can come to you if you need any help.

Determining If Students Can Process New Information Using Reciprocal Teaching

Monitoring should always have two components: 1) something that students do to demonstrate the desired result of the technique (in this instance, process new information using the RT technique) and 2) something that the teacher does to check for the desired results and respond to the students' progress. Here are two specific examples of monitoring that flow from the use of this technique:

- The teacher listens to each collaborative group to monitor students' understanding of new information and their degree of collaboration with peers.

- The teacher asks students to create an independent summary to hand in as they exit the classroom.

Table 5.5 is a student proficiency scale to assess your students' progress toward proficiency in using the RT method.

Table 5.5: Scale for Monitoring the Use of Reciprocal Teaching

Emerging	Fundamental	Desired Result
Students make predictions about future information.	Students make predictions about future information by drawing conclusions, then testing their inferences.	Students make predictions about future information by drawing conclusions, then testing their inferences and readjusting their prediction when necessary.
Students summarize the information.	Students summarize the main idea of the information.	Students summarize the main idea of the information by explaining the critical information.
Students engage in a self-evaluation of their comprehension of the content.	Students identify specific areas in which their thinking is off track.	Students make adjustments to get back on track with their thinking if they discover their thinking is off track.
Students generate questions about content.	Students generate questions about significant content.	Students generate questions that self-test their understanding about significant content.

Scaffold and Extend Instruction to Meet Students' Needs

You will no doubt have students in your classroom who need either extra help or enrichment of some type. Following are some ways you can scaffold and extend instruction:

Scaffolding

Here are some ways you can scaffold the RT technique:

- Ask students to think aloud to complete each step of the method.

- Divide the oral presentation or text to be read into smaller chunks.

- Ask students to read aloud to their teacher or partner when engaging in the question-generating section of the method.

- Provide secondary resources based on student fluency levels and comprehension levels.

- Group students with similar learning needs, and remain with the group during the *previewing, question-generating,* and *clarification* steps of the method.

- Use primary resources that have several pictures or models to enhance the spoken or written explanations.

- Provide a written copy of the steps of the method.

- Provide sources in different forms: videos, audio clips, and so on.

Extending

Here are examples of some ways you can extend instruction for those students who are able to move ahead more quickly:

- Have students research their own secondary resources to use to further substantiate their summaries.

- Invite students to create graphic representation of their summaries or conclusions.

- Have them create a tech-savvy representation of their summaries or conclusions.

- Provide primary resources commensurate with the learners' advanced reading fluency and comprehension levels.

- Ask students to assist the teacher during the clarification step of the method.

Instructional Technique 6

USING SCRIPTED COOPERATIVE DYADS

Scripted Cooperative Dyads were originally developed as a processing technique for college students who had great difficulties with reading, understanding, and retaining new information from their textbooks (Dansereau, 1988). However, it can easily be adapted for younger students to actively process information during partner reading of content text. The critical attribute of this process is that, when used over time, it disciplines students to become more attentive and accountable for their recalling and summarizing of critical new information. The process is most helpful for older elementary and secondary students who are gradually expected to understand and retain increasing amounts of critical content.

How to Effectively Implement the Processing of New Information Using Scripted Cooperative Dyads

In contrast to other techniques in which students are expected to play various roles, Scripted Cooperative Dyads have only two roles: recaller and listener. Table 6.1 enumerates the steps in this technique when students are cooperatively reading new text.

Table 6.1: Steps in the Technique When Students Are Cooperatively Reading New Text

Steps in the Technique	Explanatory Notes for the Teacher
1. The teacher explains and models the two roles that students will take turns playing—recaller and listener—as they cooperatively read an assignment in their textbook.	Before implementing this technique, choose easier reading text until students have acquired the two roles.
2. Both students read the text chorally or silently and jot down central ideas and key details as they read.	There are two ways you can approach the reading process depending on the reading levels and proficiencies of your students. Students who can read grade-level textbooks with good comprehension can read text silently. However, partner whisper reading in which both readers articulate the words together can be helpful, as the stronger reader can keep the process moving.
3. The recaller summarizes the new information orally for the listener without looking at any of his written notes.	If students are reading silently, the person who finishes first should go back and review/reread until the partner catches up.
4. The listener listens carefully to discover any errors or omissions. The listener can refer to his notes when listening to the summary.	If the listener hears any wrong information, he can politely interrupt the recaller to correct him.
5. The recaller summarizes as rapidly as he can, trying to include all the important ideas and facts.	The recaller draws a picture or diagram if he desires. The summary has to be in his own words, not the author's.
6. The listener provides feedback to the recaller on errors, distortions, and the material he omitted.	The listener should then look at the passage and do the following things: See if he can help his partner remember any of the new information by coming up with some clever ways to memorize important facts or ideas. The goal is that both the recaller and listener will thoroughly process the new content.
7. Together the partners elaborate on the material presented—they develop analogies, generate images, relate the new information to prior knowledge, or reformat the material. The script is formalized in a think sheet that keeps student partners on task and ensures meaningful processing takes place.	With older students, this process will constitute active processing at its finest. The partners can keep on discussing things they have learned even after class ends.

Table 6.2 presents a streamlined version of the steps in the Scripted Cooperative Dyads process that you could provide to students as a guide during their first few uses of the process.

Table 6.2: Steps in the Scripted Cooperative Dyads Process

Reading Goal	Determine Two or More Main Ideas of the Text, Explain How They Are Supported by Details, and Summarize the Text
1. Pair	"Write your name and the name of your partner on your think sheet. The person whose birthday comes first in the calendar year will be the recaller."
2. Read	"Read the first chunk of text independently."
3. Write	"Jot down some key words and phrases that will remind you of the main idea of the first chunk of text."
4. Recall	"Recaller: First, put away your notes. Then, summarize from memory what you have read."
5. Listen	"Listener: Use your notes to provide feedback on errors or any important ideas that the recaller forgot."
After reading the next chunk of information, students exchange roles. The recaller becomes the listener, and the listener becomes the recaller.	
After completing the Read/Write/Recall/Listen steps for the remaining two chunks of text, the partners move to the final step: Summarize.	
6. Summarize	The partners work together to satisfy the reading goal by writing two or more main ideas of the text, explaining how they are supported by details, and writing a summary statement.

Adapted from McEwan-Adkins (2010).

Examples and Nonexamples of Processing New Information Using Scripted Cooperative Dyads

Following are two sets of examples and nonexamples, one from elementary classrooms and another from secondary classrooms.

Elementary Example of Processing New Information
Using Scripted Cooperative Dyads

The learning target for the elementary example is *determine two or more main ideas of a text and explain how they are supported by key details; summarize the text* (CCSS.ELA-Literacy.RI.5.2).

The fifth-grade teacher in this example knows that her students need more practice processing new content text independently and believes that using the Scripted Cooperative Dyads method will give students the structure they need to process text with a partner immediately after they read it. She explains the purpose of using the method:

> Class, today we're going to learn a collaborative reading process. You will pair up with a partner and read science or social studies text on your own. Then, each of you will choose a part to play—recaller or listener. Each partner will get a chance to play each role.

The teacher decides to slightly vary the format found in Table 6.2. She will chunk the text she has chosen for students to read into three parts, but she will read aloud the first chunk and model the process with a student volunteer. She gives the student a copy of the streamlined process modified to reflect that she will read the first chunk aloud. The student volunteer decides to be the listener, and the teacher is the recaller.

She reminds her students that even though she and the volunteer are modeling the process, the rest of the class should pay close attention as she reads aloud. They should think about the notes they might take about the main idea or details if they were helping her. After reading the first chunk of text aloud and taking notes, the teacher and the student volunteer assume their roles. The teacher lists several details from the text, leaving out one or two things that she should have included. The student volunteer is the listener and gets to use his notes to remind the teacher about what she has forgotten. The teacher asks the class if they have any additional ideas, and two people add more details. Then the teacher and the volunteer read the goal: "Determine two or more main ideas of the text, explain how they are supported by details, and summarize the text." Together, the teacher and volunteer settle on two main ideas and come up with supporting details for them. Then, they write a summary together.

The teacher directs the class to pair up with their preassigned partners and get ready to read:

> Class, now it's your turn to try collaborative reading. Remember, the person whose birthday comes first in the year will be the recaller, and the other person will be the listener. But, on the last chunk, you switch with each other. Remember as you're reading and taking notes to listen so you can recall.

The collaborative reading process exceeds the teacher's expectations. She is excited to see her students talking with a partner about what they have read and decides to use the process once a week to engage students in the reading of content text.

Elementary Nonexample of Processing New Information Using Scripted Cooperative Dyads

The learning target for the elementary nonexample is *determine two or more main ideas of a text and explain how they are supported by key details; summarize the text* (CCSS.ELA-Literacy.RI.5.2).

The fifth-grade teacher feels the pressure to engage his students in the active processing of new informational text and decides to use the Scripted Cooperative Dyads method. The process seems pretty straightforward to him, and since he is pressed for time with all of the standards he needs to cover, he decides to skip all the explaining and modeling and just go forward with a brief explanation. His students have done collaborative processing in the past, and he believes they will catch right on to this process. However, keeping track of the two roles and who is supposed to do what gets a bit confusing. Since the students do not have an opportunity to walk through it and see it modeled, they get bogged down in the details of the process and do not have time to focus on the active processing of new information.

Secondary Example of Processing New Information
Using Scripted Cooperative Dyads

The learning target for the secondary example is *read closely to deter-mine what the text says explicitly; cite specific textual evidence when writing or speaking to support conclusions from the text* (CCR Readiness Anchor Standards for Reading, Grades 6–12).

A social studies teacher is concerned about the number of students in his classes who do not seem to be completing the assigned chapters in their text-book. He knows something has to be done since more than half of his class failed the last quiz over the chapter. He decides to use the Scripted Coopera-tive Dyads method to give his students an incentive for getting a study buddy to read the chapters. He teaches students the process, walks through it with several different student volunteers, and guarantees that if they use the pro-cess with a study buddy for the coming week's chapter, they will get an *A* on the quiz. Just to prove to his students that this process really works, he offers them an opportunity to retake a different version of the quiz *after* they use the process to read and process last week's chapter. His students are intrigued, and about half of them take him up on his offer.

He is counting on this process to work and develops a new version of the quiz. To his and the students' great surprise, out of the fourteen students who previously failed the quiz since they did not sufficiently understand and retain the new information, twelve of them ace the new quiz, and the other two admit they have skipped using the process. The teacher plans to give stu-dents an in-class study period to use the process to see how the whole class results turn out. He is motivated enough to promise that if 90 percent of the students get an *A* on the quiz, he will treat the entire class to pizza and soda.

Secondary Nonexample of Processing New
Information Using Scripted Cooperative Dyads

The learning target for the secondary nonexample is *read closely to deter-mine what the text says explicitly; cite specific textual evidence when writing or speaking to support conclusions from the text* (CCR Readiness Anchor Standards for Reading, Grades 6–12).

The secondary nonexample teacher has similar concerns about his students' ability to process new information from their content texts. The

Scripted Cooperative Dyads method also intrigues him. He likes the idea that it was originally developed for college students who were having problems similar to the ones he encounters with his students. He feels he cannot take regular class time to teach it to his students and decides to offer an after-school tutoring session for students who are interested in raising their grades on weekly quizzes. He gets a very poor turnout at the after-school session and is so discouraged by it that he tells the six students who have come that he is going to reschedule it for another time when more students can attend. The teacher's lack of commitment to the process shows in two ways: his unwillingness to use any of his lecture time for processing activities and his lack of consideration for the six students who attended the tutoring session. They represented one-third of his class and could have easily become his poster students for the process.

Determining If Students Can Process New Information Using Scripted Cooperative Dyads

Monitoring students' abilities to process new information from content text using Scripted Cooperative Dyads can easily be accomplished with one of these tasks:

- The teacher requires that students hand in their processing notes and summative conclusions after completing their collaborative processing of content text.

- The teacher creates ten-item quizzes that assess students' mastery of the critical content.

- The teacher listens in to each collaborative group during in-class collaborative processing to monitor students' understanding of new information and their degree of collaboration with peers.

Table 6.3 is a student proficiency scale to assess your students' progress toward proficiency in processing new information using Scripted Cooperative Dyads.

Table 6.3: Proficiency Scale for Monitoring the Processing of New Information Using Scripted Cooperative Dyads

Emerging	Fundamental	Desired Result
Students identify ideas and details.	Students identify the central idea and key details.	Students identify the central idea and key details that support it.
Students summarize new information.	Students summarize new information including important ideas and facts.	Students summarize new information including important ideas and how facts support them.
Students provide feedback to their partners regarding errors, distortions, or material their partners omitted.	Students generate specific feedback to partners regarding errors, distortions, and material their partners omitted.	Students generate specific feedback to partners that helps the partner correct the mistake.
Students elaborate on material.	Students elaborate on material and justify their elaboration.	Students are able to elaborate on content in multiple ways.

Scaffold and Extend Instruction to Meet Students' Needs

You may have students in your classroom who need either extra help or enrichment of some type. Following are some ways you can scaffold and extend instruction.

Scaffolding

Here are some ways you can scaffold the Scripted Cooperative Dyads method:

- Prepare think sheets or wall charts to remind students of how the process works.

- Divide the text to be read into smaller chunks.

- Provide secondary resources based on student fluency levels and comprehension levels for student pairs whose reading skills need support.

- Pair students with similar learning needs, and remain with this larger group to facilitate the process more directly.

Extending

Here are examples of some ways you can extend instruction for those students who are able to move ahead more quickly:

- Come up with unique ways to represent critical content to make it more memorable.

- Create graphic representation of their summaries or conclusions.

- Create a tech-savvy representation of their summaries or conclusions.

- Provide primary resources commensurate with the learners' advanced reading fluency and comprehension levels.

Conclusion

The goal of this guide is to enable teachers to become more effective in teaching content to their students. The beginning step, as you have learned in the preceding pages, is to become skilled at helping your students *process new information*.

To determine if this goal has been met, you will need to gather information from students, as well as solicit feedback from your supervisor or colleagues, to find someone willing to embark on this learning journey with you. Engage in a meaningful self-reflection on your use of the strategy. If you acquire nothing else from this book, let it be the importance of *monitoring*. The tipping point in your level of expertise and your students' achievement is *monitoring*. Implementing this strategy well is not enough. Your goal is the desired result: evidence that your students have developed a deeper understanding of the content.

To be most effective, view implementation as a three-step process:

1. Implement the strategy using your energy and creativity to adopt and adapt the various techniques in this guide.

2. Monitor for the desired result. In other words, while you are implementing the technique, determine whether that technique is effective with the students. Check in real time to immediately see or hear whether your students are processing new information through meaningful discussions with peers, asking questions of other students, and giving and writing summaries of the new information.

3. If, as a result of your monitoring, you realize that your instruction was not adequate for students to achieve the desired result, seek out ways to change and adapt.

Although you can certainly experience this guide and gain expertise independently, the process will be more beneficial if you read and work through its contents with colleagues.

Reflection and Discussion Questions

Use the following reflection and discussion questions during a team meeting or even as food for thought prior to a meeting with your coach, mentor, or supervisor:

1. How has your instruction changed as a result of reading and implementing the instructional techniques found in this book?

2. What ways have you found to modify and enhance the instructional techniques found in this book to scaffold and extend your instruction?

3. What was your biggest challenge, in terms of implementing this instructional strategy?

4. How would you describe the changes in your students' learning that have occurred as a result of implementing this instructional strategy?

5. What will you do to share what you have learned with colleagues at your grade level or in your department?

References

Aronson, E., & Patnoe, S. (2011). *Cooperation in the classroom: The jigsaw method.* London: Printer & Martin.

Bruner, J. (1973) *Going Beyond the Information Given.* New York: Norton.

Common Core State Standards Initiative. (2014). *Preparing America's students for success.* Retrieved February 14, 2014, from http://www.corestandards.org

Dansereau, D. F. (1988). Cooperative learning strategies. In C. E. Weinstein, E. T. Goetz, & P. A. Alexander (Eds.), *Learning and study strategies: Issues in assessment, instruction, and evaluation* (pp. 103–120). New York: Academic Press.

Dickson, S. V., Collins, V. L., Simmons, D. C., & Kame'enui, E. J. (1998). Metacognitive strategies: Instructional curricular basics and implications. In D. C. Simmons & E. J. Kame'enui (Eds.), *What reading research tells us about children with diverse learning needs* (pp. 361–380). Hillsdale, NJ: Erlbaum.

Fisher, D., Frey, N., & Lapp, D. (2012). *Teaching students to read like detectives: Comprehending, analyzing, and discussing text.* Bloomington, IN: Solution Tree Press.

Johnson, D., Maruyama, G., Johnson, R., Nelson, D., & Skon, L. (1981). Effects of cooperative, competitive, and individualistic goal structures on achievement: A meta-analysis. *Psychological Bulletin, 89*(1), 47–62.

Joyce, B., & Weil, M. (1986). *Models of teaching* (3rd ed.). Englewood Cliffs, NJ: Prentice Hall.

Ledwith, J. (2014). What is a system of linear equations? *About Education.* Retrieved November 16, 2014, from http://math.about.com/od/linearequations/tp/Syst_Lin-1.htm

Lyman, F. T. (1981). The responsive classroom discussion: The inclusion of all students. *Mainstreaming Digest,* pp. 109–113. College Park: University of Maryland Press.

Marzano, R. J. (2007). *The art and science of teaching: A comprehensive framework for effective instruction.* Alexandria, VA: Association for Supervision and Curriculum Development.

Marzano, R., & Boogren, T. (2012). *Strategies for reflective practice.* Denver, CO: Marzano Research Laboratory.

Marzano, R. J., & Toth, M. D. (2013). *Deliberate practice for deliberate growth: Teacher evaluation systems for continuous instructional improvement*. West Palm Beach, FL: Learning Sciences International.

The Math Forum. (2002). Different ways of solving systems of linear equations. *Ask Dr. Math*, October 28. Retrieved November 1, 2014, from http://mathforum.org /library/drmath/view/61608.html

McEwan, E. K. (2007). *40 ways to support struggling readers in content classrooms, grades 6–12*. Thousand Oaks, CA: Corwin.

McEwan, E. K., & Bresnahan, V. (2008). *Vocabulary, grades 4–8*. Thousand Oaks, CA: Corwin.

McEwan-Adkins, E. K. (2010). *40 reading intervention strategies: Research-based support for RTI*. Bloomington, IN: Solution Tree Press.

McEwan-Adkins, E. K., & Burnett, A. J. (2012). *20 literacy strategies to meet the Common Core: Increasing rigor in middle and high school classrooms*. Bloomington, IN: Solution Tree Press.

McEwan, E. K., Dobberteen, K. W., & Pearce, Q. L. (2008). *The reading puzzle: Fluency, grades 4–8*. Thousand Oaks, CA: Corwin.

Palinscar, A., & Brown, A. L. (1984). Reciprocal teaching of comprehension-fostering and comprehension-monitoring activities. *Cognition and Instruction, 1*(2), 117–175.

Rasinski, T. V., & Padak, N. (2000). *Effective reading strategies: Teaching children who find reading difficult* (2nd ed.). Upper Saddle River, NJ: Merrill.

Strong, R. W., Silver, H. F., Perini, M. J., & Tuculescu, G. M. (2002). *Reading for academic success: Powerful strategies for struggling, average, and advanced readers, grades 7–12*. Thousand Oaks, CA: Corwin.

Walberg, H. J. (1999). Productive teaching. In H. C. Waxman & H. J. Walberg (Eds.), *New directions for teaching practice research* (pp. 75–104). Berkeley, CA: McCutchen.

Index

A

A-B-C- triad for processing new information, 20

Aronson, E., 61

Art and Science of Teaching, The (Marzano), 19

attribute, defined, 50

B

Boogren, T., 79–81

Brown, A. L., 75, 79

Bruner, J., 52

C

CCR (College and Career Readiness) Anchor Standards, defined, 2

CCSS (Common Core State Standards), 3 defined, 2

CCSSI (Common Core State Standards Initiative), defined, 2

clarifying, 77, 78

collaboration, use of term, 14

collaborative processing

  See also cooperative learning

  benefits of, 14

  common mistakes, avoiding, 21

  description of technique, 13

  directions, giving, 16–17

  examples and nonexamples, 21–26

  explaining, 16

  facilitating, 18–19

  implementation, 13–20

  modeling/summarizing, 17–18

  monitoring for desired result, 26–27

  scaffolding and extending instruction, 28

  student proficiency scale, 27

  teaching behaviors needed for, 15–20

  what, why, when, and how of, 14–15

concept, defined, 50

concept attainment

  common mistakes, avoiding, 54

  description of technique, 49

  examples and nonexamples, 55–58

  implementation, 49–54

  Ins and Outs, 49, 57–58

  lesson steps for, 51–52, 53–54

  monitoring for desired result, 59

  scaffolding and extending instruction, 60

  student proficiency scale, 59

  vocabulary for, 50

cooperative learning

  See also collaborative processing

  defined, 13

  difference between group work and, 13

D

declarative knowledge/information, 19–20

defining attribute, defined, 50

desired result

  See also name of instructional technique

  defined, 2

directions, giving, 16–17

directly instructing, 14–15

MARZANO CENTER

Essentials for Achieving Rigor SERIES

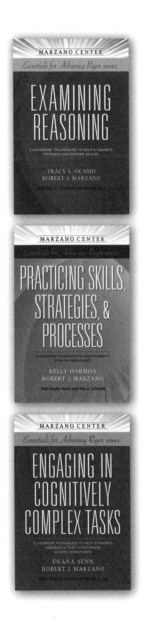

EXAMINING REASONING
Classroom Techniques to Help Students Produce and Defend Claims
TRACY L. OCASIO
ROBERT J. MARZANO
With Ria A. Schmidt and Deana Senn

PRACTICING SKILLS, STRATEGIES, & PROCESSES
Classroom Techniques to Help Students Develop Proficiency
KELLY HARMON
ROBERT J. MARZANO
With Kathy Marx and Ria A. Schmidt

ENGAGING IN COGNITIVELY COMPLEX TASKS
Classroom Techniques to Help Students Generate & Test Hypotheses Across Disciplines
DEANA SENN
ROBERT J. MARZANO
With Tracy L. Ocasio and Barry L. Sift

IDENTIFYING CRITICAL CONTENT
Classroom Techniques to Help Students Know What Is Important
DEANA SENN
AMBER C. RUTHERFORD
ROBERT J. MARZANO

EXAMINING SIMILARITIES & DIFFERENCES
Classroom Techniques to Help Students Deepen Their Understanding
CONNIE SCOLES WEST
ROBERT J. MARZANO
With Carla Marx and Patricia L. Sift

PROCESSING NEW INFORMATION
Classroom Techniques to Help Students Engage with Content
T ZEFORAW SAHADEO-TURNER
ROBERT J. MARZANO
With Gwendolyn L. Bryant and Kelly Harmon

Creating & Using LEARNING TARGETS & PERFORMANCE SCALES
How Teachers Make Better Instructional Decisions
CARLA MOORE
LIBBY H. GARST
ROBERT J. MARZANO
With Elizabeth Kennedy and Deana Senn

RECORDING & REPRESENTING KNOWLEDGE
Classroom Techniques to Help Students
RIA A. SCHMIDT
ROBERT J. MARZANO
With Libby H. Garst and Laurine Halter

REVISING KNOWLEDGE
Classroom Techniques to Help Students Examine Their Deeper Understanding
RIA A. SCHMIDT
ROBERT J. MARZANO
With Laurine Halter, Tracy L. Ocasio, and Deana Senn

ORGANIZING FOR LEARNING
Classroom Techniques to Help Students Interact Within Small Groups
DEANA SENN
ROBERT J. MARZANO
With Libby H. Garst and Carla Moore

Learning Sciences International
LEARNING AND PERFORMANCE MANAGEMENT

Visit www.education-store.learningsciences.com or call 877-411-7114